WINDOW ON MOUNT ZION

WINDOW
ON MOUNT ZION

Pauline Rose

SOUTH BRUNSWICK AND NEW YORK:
A. S. Barnes and Company
1973

First American edition, 1973.
Library of Congress Catalog
Card Number: 72-12446

A. S. Barnes and Co., Inc
Cranbury, New Jersey 08512

ISBN 0-498-01342-1

Printed in Great Britain

74-126

CONTENTS

CONTENTS

To Albert

Beautiful for situation,
the joy of the whole earth,
is Mount Zion.
On the sides of the north,
the city of the great King.

Psalm 48

Chapter One

I came on my first visit to this land in 1946, and when I reached Jerusalem something seemed to stir in the depths of my being. I felt that all the journeying and searching of my life had come to an end. Jerusalem held out its golden, welcoming arms to me.

We were living in London at that time, and in 1947, against everyone's advice and pleading I felt a compelling urge to return to Jerusalem to share in the birth pains of the State of Israel.

The hardships of the Siege of Jerusalem were not easy for any of us, citizen and visitor alike; but where one is bound by love there is no burden too heavy to bear and no suffering too great to endure. Jerusalem held me in an ever-tightening embrace.

I came from London for some months in each of the following years, until finally in 1959 Albert, my husband, and I were able to leave London to settle in Israel.

For four years we lived in temporary homes, knowing that we had not yet found our real home. There was no doubt in our minds that it was going to be in Jerusalem—but where? And what purpose would there be to our lives? I knew there was something I had to do beyond settling down to a pleasant and comfortable personal life. I waited for some inner guidance.

One day I visited my friend Malla, who lived in Tel Aviv and is the sister of Dr Kahane, the Curator of Mount Zion. I had known the family since 1946. Malla had visited us when we were living on a farm in a London suburb, and had never forgotten the beautiful garden we had had there.

As we sat reminiscing, she suddenly looked at me and said: 'Why don't you go and make a garden on Mount Zion?'

It seemed an incredible suggestion and I smiled.

'How would that be possible? I'd never be allowed to do anything on Mount Zion; and besides, it's a military border zone.'

'Go and talk to my brother,' she said, and then the conversation turned to other subjects. It was like a flash which gave momentary light, disappearing almost immediately. But for the next few days and nights the words haunted me and left me no peace. *Go and make a garden on Mount Zion.*

The vision of Mount Zion and the Biblical prophecies for its future were always specially illuminated in my mind, but I had no personal connection with it. The phrase linked itself to a verse in Isaiah which speaks of the beautifying of the sanctuary of the Lord. Surely, I thought, this sanctuary must be Mount Zion, for '*The Lord said: "here is my rest for ever, here will I dwell, for I have desired it".*'

I could not rest—I had to go to Mount Zion.

On Mount Zion

'*Walk about Mount Zion*', said David in his psalm. '*Walk about her, go around her.*' This I set out to do and came to the foot of the Mount.

A stone path, with winding steps between green shrubs and bushes, was then the only means of ascent for pilgrims and visitors to Mount Zion. A heavily padlocked barrier barred the approach to a military track which went around the Hill.

On this day, I slowly and meditatively climbed the steps. I passed the notice board requesting men and women to be suitably dressed and to have their heads covered when visiting this holy Hill. On the way up were other notice boards bearing quotations from the Psalms:

> 'Give thanks unto the name of the Lord.
> For there are set the seats of judgement,
> The seats of the house of David.
> Pray for the peace of Jerusalem.'

> 'The Lord is great in Zion. He is high above all the people.'

At the summit, facing the new City of Jerusalem, stood a large, old, tarnished menorah (eight-branched candlestick) with its twisted arms outstretched; the 'Flying Menorah' which legend claims is the one that Titus took from the Temple and placed on an arch in Rome. There, suffering, it waited through the centuries to return to its proper place—the Temple on Mount Moriah. When the State of Israel was established it received wings and flew back to Jerusalem, seeking the Temple. Finding only a mosque with a golden dome in its place, it rested on Mount Zion, where it still waits to return to Mount Moriah.

Beyond this menorah, a little forest of pine trees, bent by the storms of ages, gave shade in an open space. They, too, seemed to be waiting—waiting for the day that Mount Zion would be restored to its former glory.

To the left, a high stone wall enclosed the grounds belonging to the Dormition Church. To the right was a large, rambling, deserted building, the great open gashes in its walls roughly filled with stones and débris, its roof a skeleton. The former Bishop Gobart School for Arab Boys, it had stood decaying since the battles of 1948.

Ahead was a signboard. 'DANGER. NO ENTRY. MILITARY ZONE.' Behind the wall ahead stood a large stone house bearing the scars of a past war and evidence of preparedness for a future one. The bricked-up windows, sandbags and gun emplacements identified it as the Mount Zion military post.

I sat on a bench beneath the branches of the old pine trees. It seemed as if time was momentarily suspended. There was a strange silence, a stillness vibrating with the echoes of past cries and future songs, spanning the centuries of Israel's history from the time of King David. Somewhere near here, King David had conquered the Jebusites, had taken the castle of Zion and built the City of David.

A deep peace pervaded the whole scene. A peace born of prayers that lingered and tears that had spent themselves. A peace deep in the heart of Mount Zion, assured of its glorious future.

Then I wandered through the old, vaulted building which according to tradition houses the tomb of King David— the magnet drawing the pilgrims. Part of this building had been restored, but the countless rooms above it were still in ruins.

The Obstacles

Where could I make a garden? How could I get permission to live on Mount Zion? I revealed my thoughts and desires to Dr Kahane. While he sympathized with them, he was gravely concerned for our physical safety, and doubted that his committee would approve or that the military authorities, who also had a say in the matter, would give permission.

'There's no need to make a garden, and nobody is allowed to live here. It is after all a holy sanctuary, and also a dangerous place under present conditions—a border zone. It really isn't a place for anyone to live.' He was silent a while. Then, 'Impossible! Quite impossible!' he said with conviction, and with that he considered the matter closed.

I could not accept this as the last word; the matter was not ended in my mind! To man many things are impossible, but to God all things are possible. Both Albert and I felt that if the inspiration to come to Mount Zion was from God, the impossible might well become possible. We waited.

We were faced with two tremendous obstacles: permission to live on Mount Zion and permission to use the military road. To live here, without being allowed to use the road, would be difficult in the extreme. The steps up to Mount Zion would be our only means of access; everything we needed would have to be hauled up on the backs of donkeys.

There were endless discussions with the patient Curator, and it seemed to me that the ever-repeated 'impossible' was beginning to ring with less conviction. The first break was an offer of a small piece of ground to make a garden.

Then I was allowed to have a room where I might rest, or occasionally spend the night when working on the garden. Of course, it was clearly understood that I could not live there, and there was always the condition that garden or room had to be on the 'safe side' of Mount Zion, the side that did not face the border.

I was grateful for *any* foothold on Mount Zion. We looked for garden sites and rooms, but each time we found something that appeared to be suitable we uncovered some hidden snag. However, if we were to be allowed to come to Mount Zion at all, then we believed that all our steps and plans would be guided by the same power that had brought us there. Somewhere on Mount Zion we would find the place intended for us.

The next problem to be faced was how to get permission to use the military road. Our first enquiries met with another 'impossible'. The road was strictly for military use and nobody else could be given a key with which to unlock the barrier.

The Military Commander of Jerusalem said to us: 'It's an extremely foolish idea to want to live in such a dangerous, isolated place, when it's not necessary.' It was very difficult to explain to him my reasons and the faith underlying them. Again we waited.

Long weeks passed without a decision. Would we get

permission or not? Somehow I knew I had only to wait and I was willing to do so. Then one day, without explanation, we received the key to the barrier and permission from the army to use the road. . . .

Now the confirmation was complete and the vision had become clearer. We had only to find the place where we could live and also make a garden.

Now we had the key and could take the car on the military road. As we reached the foot of the hill, a forbidding iron bar secured by a heavy padlock stretched across the only road leading to the top of Mount Zion. was conscious of my excitement and a strong sense of responsibility as I turned the key in the padlock, releasing the giant iron arm which opened the way for the car to pass through. At last I stood on the forbidden road. Conscientiously, I locked the barrier behind me with the key which had been given to us on condition that it should never pass from our hands.

The road was a rough track cut out of the side of the Mount for the use of military vehicles. It was dangerously narrow and heavily pot-holed and treacherous for a small car, and it curved and climbed sharply with the contours of the hill. But this was not all. On one side the hill rose high to its stone-walled summit; on the other, it sloped sharply down to the valley of Hinnom. The first curve brought the enemy gunpost on the opposite hill alarmingly close, and the armed Arab guards scrutinizing all movement could be clearly seen.

With great difficulty the car climbed the narrow track avoiding large stones and the deep furrows left by the daily quota of heavy military traffic. Almost at the summit, a sharp bend revealed the breathtaking vista of the Judean Hills, the hills of Biblical history. But it was not the moment to contemplate scenic beauty—my head was suddenly and painfully banged against the roof of the car as it lurched into an unseen hole in the road. A few more yards of climbing and the possibility of further driving ended. I had stopped the car before a yellow signboard on which was written: 'DANGER. FRONTIER AHEAD.' And there was another fortification occupied by Jordanian soldiers some yards behind this.

High on the hill stood the house occupied by our soldiers —our defence post. Around it were ruined houses left damaged and derelict after the War of Liberation in 1948. My attention was drawn to one in the foreground on the top of the Mount. It faced the Jordanian border, scarcely a hundred yards away, and it seemed to stand like a silent stone sentinel guarding Mount Zion, its windows looking east, west and south. It seemed to be calling for life to enter its empty shell, heal its ugly war scars and light up its darkened windows.

I left the car and walked up to the summit of the Mount. Nobody was in sight. The stone house I had seen from below was in ruins. Not far off, flanking an old wall, was a tiny primitive-looking garden. The fluttering wings of pigeons circled the badly war-damaged house.

* * *

Through masses of débris and stones, I risked jumps over small craters, and managed to make a precarious entry into the house. I went through a doorway, the damaged doors hanging from their frames, crossed gaps in the floor from which the tiles had been removed, and found my way to the staircase which had remained intact. I walked up to the floor above, pushed my way into the room facing the border, and there had my first glimpse through a window on Mount Zion.

I stepped on to a small balcony with no certainty that it would hold me. The picture which opened out before me was like a great canvas stretching through time and space. The Judean Hills between the Mount of Olives and the Hill of Evil Counsel sloped into the valley of Kidron, which in turn wound around the foot of the mountains and was then lost to view on its way to Ein Gedi on the Dead Sea.

The little stone houses of the Arab village of Silwan, nestling on the hillside, looked as if they had grown out of the rock. Hidden among the trees on the Hill of Evil Counsel was the building housing the United Nations personnel. A golden glow was diffused over hill and valley alike and was reflected in the misty blues, mauves and yellows of the distant mountains of Moab, rising beyond the Dead Sea. Peace and stillness spread like a cloak over the landscape and it was hard to believe that the enemy was hidden in its folds, and that if I took only a few steps beyond the sign marked 'DANGER. FRONTIER AHEAD', I should be shot or taken prisoner.

Inside the house, bullet-riddled walls, broken doors, sandbags, dirt, all told their story. How many young lives had been lost? How many men had been hurt or maimed in the battles for Israel's independence fought from this house? As I was trying to push open a tightly closed door I heard footsteps on the stairs. A small, thin, elderly man appeared; smiling black eyes in a dark-skinned, wrinkled face looked at me with questioning surprise.

'Who are you?' I asked.

'I am Obadiah,' he replied. 'I work on Mount Zion and look after the plants and pigeons.' He seemed puzzled by my presence.

'I was curious to see the inside of this house,' I explained. 'Where do you come from, Obadiah?'

'From Yemen,' he answered. 'I came here ten years ago with my wife and our seven children. I was not strong enough for full-time work, so they gave me light work on Mount Zion. Praised be the Name.' He looked upwards with shining eyes. It was as though a prayer of thanksgiving was released from his heart and ascended heavenwards.

A strange noise could be heard inside the room behind the closed door.

'Would you like to see?' asked Obadiah.

He lifted a bar across the door and beckoned me closer. Gently he pushed the door open and I was startled by a great fluttering of wings. We entered the Mount Zion pigeon sanctuary, guarded, cared for and protected by Obadiah.

He spoke softly to the birds in a language which they seemed to understand. He took out of his pocket a handful of grain and they alighted on his arms, his shoulders and his dark, curly head. Obadiah's face beamed with pleasure. He pointed to the structures on the walls: 'I made these for the pigeons to nest in,' he said. 'I have been looking after them and feeding them for the past ten years. There were only a few when I came.' He smiled. 'Now there is hardly room enough for them.'

Birds with their young had made their own nests on the floor all around the side of the walls. The room was filled with fluttering wings.

We left the birds to their peaceful, undisturbed life and Obadiah fastened the door securely behind us. He showed me other rooms, all in the same state of ruin and neglect. Then he led me down the stairs and showed me a less dangerous way out of the house. As we walked in the direction of David's tomb he proudly showed me his little garden. A few rose-bushes were making a great effort to survive between geraniums and other more hardy shrubs. There was ample evidence of his loving care.

I recalled the words of one of Israel's prophets foretelling this spirit of kindness: '*They shall not hurt or destroy in all my holy mountain*', and I realized that a ray of the light of Mount Zion had touched the heart of Obadiah. Was this not the house in which those rays of light could shine ever brighter, so that not only birds and flowers but also people could experience this spirit of kindness?

B

A strong sense of conviction grew in me that this was the house I was looking for.

* * *

When, some days later, I expressed my desire to live in this derelict house right on the border, everyone was shocked at the idea.

'Absolutely out of the question!' said Dr Kahane. 'Forget all about it!'

However, my conviction remained strong. And it was not long after that we received, to our complete surprise, a list of conditions which would have to be observed if we were to live in this house on Mount Zion.

We were to understand fully the dangers and risks, and accept entire responsibility for anything that might happen to us. We could not expect any help in the reconstruction of the building or in obtaining amenities such as light and water. We were to be prepared for any contingency. We might be asked to leave the house any time, even after it had been completed and we were already living there. In addition, since the house stood in a military zone, the army had the right to evacuate us without prior notice.

Our sober-minded friends did not believe we would be insane enough, as they put it, to accept such conditions. We accepted.

* * *

An architect had promised to come and inspect the house to advise on its restoration. We arrived at the entrance to the barred road; soldiers were standing guard, and men who had just emerged from a police car were in earnest discussion with officers.

I took out my key as I approached the padlocked barrier. The soldiers, surprised to see the key in my hand, said emphatically, 'Nobody is allowed on this road today—it is not safe.'

I turned to see the architect talking to the police. His face seemed paler. A chilly wind added to our discomfort and we sensed the tension. What was happening? The rumours flew fast. We were told there were mines on the road; the Arabs were preparing some trouble—it was impossible to use the road. I turned to my companion:

'If we cannot drive up the road let us walk up the steps,' I said. 'Now that you are here, I should like you to see the house.'

He looked at me worriedly: 'Why must you think of a house on Mount Zion?' he exclaimed. 'Don't you see the danger? If it's an old Arab house you want, I can show you many in Jerusalem.'

I smiled and answered: 'I am interested in this house not because it is an old Arab house but because it stands on Mount Zion. Come up and have a look at it.'

Very reluctantly he walked up the steps with me. At the top of the Mount, the silence was broken only by the rustling of the old pine trees under which we walked. The atmosphere was oppressive. Suddenly, my companion looked at his watch, remembered an urgent appointment and quickly ran back in the direction of the steps. I never saw him again.

I walked on alone to the house. Obadiah was watering the flowers, and the pigeons flew out of the windows, one alighting on his shoulder.

The Pope's Visit

It was January 1964. The Pope had announced his intention of visiting the holy places in Israel. We were at that time planning the rebuilding of the house.

Mount Zion is sacred not only to Jews but also to Christians. Here, according to tradition, is the Coenaculum (Upper Room) where Jesus and his disciples gathered to celebrate the 'last supper'; here Mary, the mother of Jesus, is said to have fallen into her final sleep.

With the announcement of the Pope's intended visit work immediately began on the road leading to Mount Zion. After a few weeks of concentrated activity, the rough military track was transformed into a smooth asphalted road, leading to a large open space which had been cleared and surfaced to provide parking space for many cars. I called it the Pope's Parking Lot.

Immediately behind the yellow signboard marking the frontier, which stood on the east side of the square, a high, ugly, corrugated iron fence was erected to protect the Pope and his entourage and to define the Jordanian border clearly. The road continued from the Pope's Parking Lot the last few yards up the hill, to the top of the Mount where Obadiah's little garden had once flourished. It had been turned into another parking lot. The life-giving earth had been sealed off and suffocated with asphalt.

The moment I saw it I recalled the pleasure and pride with which Obadiah had shown me the few flowers he had coaxed out of the stony soil. I shared the anguish he must have felt as he watched the iron teeth of the bulldozer crush and devour the precious blooms he had nourished in order to beautify one tiny corner of Mount Zion. This parking area in front of the house I named Garden Square.

The barrier was once more lowered and locked, closing off the new road, and preparations for the Pope's arrival continued. Hundreds of security men lined the road approaching the Mount; in fact they lined the entire route from Megiddo where, early that morning, the Pope had entered Israel from Jordanian Jerusalem. After visiting the holy places around the Sea of Galilee and Nazareth, he travelled the long journey back to the Israeli side of Jerusalem. Security men were also concealed on every part of Mount Zion, since Israel was greatly concerned with the Pope's safety. No private individual was allowed within the precincts of the Mount that night.

I awaited the Pope's arrival in an observation post on an opposite hill. It was a bitterly cold night. The hour scheduled for his arrival had long passed. The wind was biting. A sudden movement along the lines of security men revived the atmosphere of expectancy and then the headlamps of police motorcycles and cars appeared in the distance travelling into the valley at the foot of Mount Zion. There they passed through the raised barrier and I watched the Pope and his entourage drive up the new road, temporarily illuminated by many floodlights. Cars filled the floodlit parking places, as the 'great father' of the Catholic Church and his companions alighted from their car in Garden Square and walked through the small gate on the way past King David's Tomb to the Upper Room.

The pigeons nesting in the room overlooking the parked cars were startled by the lights and the noise which broke the customary night silence on Mount Zion.

*   *   *

The following week, with a new key, I unlocked the new padlock which had been fitted to the barrier by the police. As our car sped smoothly up the newly made road, I was grateful to the Pope.

Now after endless difficulties and opposition, work had at last begun on the reconstruction of the house. The pigeons, so long used to it as their home, were eventually persuaded by the faithful Obadiah to transfer their home to the roof of a nearby building.

The task of reconstructing the house was completed in six months. The ordinary problems of building were increased because of the house's location. Frequent incidents on Israel's borders often necessitated the closing of the road, even to ourselves, and this interrupted the work. Each morning I had to meet the workmen and open the barrier for them; and each afternoon the ceremony was reversed.

All building supplies were similarly brought in at pre-arranged times, so that I should know when to be waiting at the barrier.

'How did you manage to get the work done so quickly?' asked a friend.

'The workmen did not feel very safe here and were anxious to complete their job as quickly as possible,' I replied. 'They worked at twice the normal speed!'

Dr Kahane visited us several times to see the progress we had made. On one occasion he looked through a broken window to see the heads of the nearby Arab soldiers above their sandbags, glanced around the room at the eight large windows and said: 'You must get bullet-proof glass for all the windows, otherwise you'll not be safe.'

'We shan't need it,' I replied.

He looked at me searchingly, as though not quite sure of my meaning.

'I'd feel better about your being here if you did this,' he said as he left.

But our windows were repaired with ordinary glass and were held in place by our faith.

*   *   *

I began to think of the need for a telephone. This was a great problem as it meant a new line to Mount Zion. The telephone department was not prepared to give it to us, even with the recommendation of the Mount Zion Committee. What were we to do?

We decided to seek the help of a doctor friend whom we had not seen for some years. He greeted us warmly.

'You both look very well,' he said. 'What can I do for you?'

'We're fine at present,' I replied, 'But we want your help concerning our well-being. We are moving to another house and since it is in rather an isolated place, we feel it is essential to have a phone.'

'Why come to me?' he asked.

'Well, supposing we need you at any time, how would we be able to contact you?'

With a friendly smile he took up his pen: 'I'll try to help,' he said. 'Where is the house?'

'On Mount Zion.'

'At what address do you want the phone?' he asked shortly.

'Mount Zion.'

He became a little impatient. 'I have no time to waste on jokes,' he said. 'If you want my help, tell me where you want your phone.'

'Mount Zion.'

He put down his pen, sat back in his chair and gave me a long look.

I answered his unspoken question. 'Yes, we're going to live on Mount Zion—right at the top, not many yards from the border.'

Another silence. Then he said: 'I certify you both as completely crazy.' He took up his pen again and wrote. . . .

Some weeks later we had a phone.

Our First Night and Day

In August 1964 the day arrived when we could occupy the house. Its war scars were healed. Lights shone again from its windows. My husband and I moved in and gave it the name Ha-Ohel (The tent). We chose this name with the prayer that the spirit of Abraham's tent would abide in it, making it a place where all people who came could find a loving welcome—a meal, a bed, rest, or renewal of the spirit, according to their needs.

Every day all over the world Jews pray: '*O cause a new light to shine upon Zion and may we all be worthy soon to enjoy its brightness.*'

We prayed that some ray of this 'new light' might shine in the home and garden we were making on Mount Zion.

*   *   *

The last glow of an August sunset was disappearing from the sky as I looked out of my window on our first evening on Mount Zion. The radiance of the stars increased as the blue of the heavens deepened. They were like tiny lighted windows in the moonless sky. On the opposite hill, occasional faint lights could be seen in the little houses of the village of Silwan. The Mount of Olives was marked only by the artificial lights outlining the arched windows of the Intercontinental Hotel.

I drew the curtains and switched on the lights. For the first time since 1948 a building on Mount Zion, so near the border, was occupied by civilians. I was conscious of the interest it aroused and had the unpleasant feeling of being watched by unseen eyes. Apart from the soldiers at the military post and the priests of the Dormition Church, we were quite alone on Mount Zion.

Before retiring for the night I had to take Tamar, our little wire-haired terrier, out for her walk. I put on her lead before we left the lighted room and went out into the darkness. I almost tripped over some stones being used to build up the entrance to the house. There was not a flicker of light to be seen anywhere, and not a sound to be heard. The darkness which seemed darker than night was sinister and hid unpleasant surprises, making familiar places unfamiliar. I was not permitted to use a torch: it would have been dangerous.

Tamar pulled at her lead, searching in this unaccustomed place for a guiding smell. I hoped she would find it quickly. Suddenly, in the darkness, I heard a rushing movement coming towards us. I grabbed Tamar in my arms as several live, panting bodies leaped on us. Tamar yelped in fear. A pack of large wild dogs nearly knocked me over as they sniffed contemptuously at Tamar, then passed on their way. Both Tamar and I were a little shaky as we returned with relief to the protection of the house. I locked the door securely behind us.

Before going to bed I opened my Bible and read: '*The Lord will create upon every dwelling place on Mount Zion, a cloud by day and the shining of a flaming fire by night. . . .*'

Comforted by the protection of this promise, I fell asleep. Soon, however, I was awakened by the mournful howling of a jackal. I lay awake listening. The animal passed beneath my window and away into the distance. Then I heard footsteps, human footsteps. I remembered the warning of the commander of the military post that there would be patrols on night duty. The footsteps receded, and again I slept, this time to be awakened by the sound of motor vehicles arriving at the military post. Mingled with these sounds were those of men's voices; soldiers speaking to each other as they carried out their duties in the darkness of the night. After a while, the rumbling of the departing vehicles trailed off into silence.

All was quiet again until a loud barking of dogs filled the air. They came across the border from Jordan in large numbers, passing the house on their nocturnal adventures.

It was that mysterious hour before the dawn, when night prepares to depart in silence as a new day is about to be born. The chanting of a man's deep, strong voice broke into the stillness. The muezzin from the top of the minaret across the border was calling his Moslem brethren to prayer —a call to draw the slumbering soul back to consciousness and awareness that his Maker had made him the gift of another day for which he must give thanks.

The first faint ray of morning light dimly outlined my curtained window. Our first night on Mount Zion had ended. Some minutes later I drew the curtains and looked through the window, welcoming the new day. I looked down at the Pope's Parking Lot on the border. On the other side of the fence I saw the heads of the Jordanian soldiers above the sandbags.

Behind the hills of Moab a red-gold light washed across the sky with the approach of day. The colour deepened as the sun appeared on the horizon, lighting the heavens and the earth with its powerful rays.

The evening and the morning of our first day.

* * *

The sun had already risen above the horizon when I left my room and Albert was reading the morning prayers. I descended the stone staircase and crossed the spacious entrance-hall where the early morning sun shone through low-arched windows. As I passed through the front entrance I saw the 'mezzuza', containing the scroll of the Law, nailed to its doorpost and I thanked God again for His Law and His Light.

I walked through the gate which opened on to Garden Square. There was not a soul about—only the pigeons and the doves on the rooftop. There was a silence and peace which belonged specifically to Mount Zion; an atmosphere heavy with memories of the past and hallowed by the prayers of centuries. The silence lingered as the shadows shortened in the sunlit square.

Suddenly I heard a voice at prayer, and I looked up. A solitary figure stood high on the roof above King David's Tomb, facing the Temple site. He poured out his soul in praise and petition to the Holy One of Israel.

The locked doors of the little museum and the Chamber of Destruction (Memorial of the Holocaust) were waiting to be opened, also the small gate leading to David's Tomb. Footsteps were coming from that direction. A key turned and the small iron gate opened. The pigeons flew down from the roof into the Square. They knew these footsteps belonged to Obadiah, who brought them their food and water each morning.

Later, the little band of Mount Zion's workers came through the small iron gate. Avraham, with his large broom, began sweeping and tidying the Square and its surroundings. The little museum, with its model of our lost Temple, opened its doors. Rabbis, guides and caretaker entered the unlocked door of the Chamber of Destruction, where grim reminders of Jewry's dark night and the unspeakable suffering of its people can be seen. Among them are the ashes of these martyrs brought to rest on Mount Zion, beside King David.

In the middle of the morning, I heard a voice proclaiming: 'You are now standing on holy Mount Zion.' Outside the house a group of American tourists were gathered around their guide listening intently to his opening remarks. He pointed to the iron fence some yards below.

'That,' he said, 'is the Jordanian border. All you see beyond that is Jordan. Those soldiers you see behind the sandbags on the rooftop are Arabs.'

Some of the women exchanged anxious glances. One said: 'Let us go back, this is a little too near the border for me.' Another, pointing to our house asked: 'Is this another museum?'

'No,' he replied, 'I think it is a private house.'

'People live here!' she exclaimed in astonishment. 'They must be crazy!'

The tourists hurriedly returned their cameras to their cases and walked back, seeking other scenes of interest.

*　　*　　*

The door bell rang. Through a window on the upper floor, I saw a stranger standing at the gate—the first visitor to Ha-Ohel. I went down to open the gate. 'Shalom,' I said, and invited him into the house.

The youthfulness of his shining blue eyes and smooth

pink cheeks was belied by his long white beard. His pockets were bulging and out of one of them he took a small well-worn Bible. He read from the Psalm of David: '*Lord who shall dwell in thy Holy Hill?*' Smiling, he said: 'You see. I had to come and find out who could be living here.'

'How did you know we were here?' I asked.

'I come to Mount Zion every day to pray. Today I heard that you had moved in.'

'You come to pray on Mount Zion every day?' I asked, amazed.

'It is the will of the Creator,' he answered, and again opened the pages of his Bible and read: '*Exalt ye the Lord our God and worship at his holy hill.*'

I realized that this was the man whose voice I had heard in prayer earlier in the morning on the roof of King David's Tomb.

Albert then entered the room looking enquiringly at the bearded stranger.

'I am Ya'acov,' he said, extending his hand to Albert. 'You must have done many "mitzvot"—good deeds—in your life for the Creator to allow you to live here.'

'No deeds that I have ever done could make me worthy to live on Mount Zion,' replied Albert.

Ya'acov read another appropriate passage from his Bible. We were to realize, when we came to know him better, that the Bibles (both English and Hebrew) that he carried around in his bulging pockets were constantly referred to. They provided him with the answer to any question, any problem, his own or someone else's. His erudition was impressive: always he unerringly turned to the relevant chapter, the appropriate verse.

'Come again,' I said to him as he prepared to leave. 'You are always welcome. Perhaps you would like to join us on the Sabbath?'

He smiled graciously, but non-committally: 'If the Creator wills,' he said as he descended the stairs.

Stones of Jerusalem

After our strange visitor had departed, I went outside and walked around the house. I was searching. Where could I make the garden—the garden on Mount Zion?

Piles of stones, rubble, remnants of walls and demolished buildings confronted me. But, I thought, how many times had the stones of Jerusalem been cast down into the dust and lifted up again? How often had the City of David been destroyed and rebuilt? How like the People of Israel were these stones? Indestructible! They were shaken out of their place, cast into the dust, broken and scattered, but never destroyed: always used again by the Master Builder for still greater glory.

The stones of Jerusalem bear silent witness to the glory of the Temple; they had walled the City and made homes for its people. Now they lay waiting for the return of the people.

Some of these ancient Jerusalem stones were mixed with untidy heaps of rubble around the house. The dust could not hide their warm glow, rose-coloured like a blush at sunrise and golden with light at sunset.

The story of Nehemiah's entry into Jerusalem to rebuild the fallen walls of the City came to my mind. He saw the destruction and he said to the few men with him: '*Come, and let us build up the wall of Jerusalem.*' *And they responded:* '*Let us rise up and build.*' *Then said Nehemiah:* '*The God of Heaven, He will prosper us, therefore we His servants will arise and build.*'

I was encouraged by these thoughts. We, too, would 'rise up and build'; with the faith of Nehemiah we would clear the rubble and use the fallen stones to repair the wall around the garden. Suddenly I had a vision: roses, lilies and myriads of coloured blooms raised their heads where the stones and dust were piled. Young trees spread blossomed branches in the fragrant air.

'*We will arise and build*' echoed in my heart as I returned to my duties in the house.

Chapter Two

First Sabbath

We were nearing the end of the week and preparing for our first Shabbat—Sabbath—on Mount Zion.

Friday morning in Israel is different from all other mornings of the week. It is marked by the increased tempo of its activities: shopping, cleaning, cooking, all work has to be finished before the Sabbath begins at sundown. On Mount Zion even greater speed was required to get through the tasks of the day because all work had to cease even earlier than in the city.

By noon, all the workers on Mount Zion were hurriedly completing their tasks, doors and gates were being locked; loitering tourists rejoined their groups and departed. Mount Zion was preparing to receive the blessing of Sabbath in silence.

As the sun moved toward the western horizon, it seemed to me as if the heavens opened and poured out upon the earth showers of winged blessings, blessings of peace, joy, rest and thankfulness—the Sabbath blessings which flow from the Most High on the seventh day.

It was as though I felt the unheard, unseen wings as they gently descended and enveloped the Holy Hill. An indescribable peace settled upon it. A peace created for all mankind, a blessing intended for every creature willing to receive it. A peace which the Eternal had ordained for the place of His habitation.

I kindled the Sabbath lights with the prayer: '*Blessed art thou O Lord our God, King of the Universe, who hast sanctified us by thine ordinances and commanded us to keep the Sabbath.*'

That evening, as always, the two synagogues on Mount Zion were closed, for it was forbidden to come to the Mount at night. Albert and I left the house, walked past the military post, entered the precincts of King David's Tomb and climbed the steps to the roof above it. From it the Old City, and particularly the Temple area, could be seen. For Jews in the divided city of Jerusalem this was the nearest point to this sacred place.

The golden dome of the Mosque of Omar (Dome of the Rock), on the Temple site, gleamed in the light of the setting sun. It dominated the Old City with its imposing size and grandeur, as though conscious of the sacredness of the rock it covered—the rock on which, according to tradition, Abraham had been prepared to sacrifice his son Isaac in obedience to God's command, and thereby laid the foundation of our faith with the promise that: *'in thy seed shall all the nations of the earth be blessed; because thou hast obeyed my voice.'*

On the wall of the Old City nearest to Mount Zion, the sandbags of a Jordanian military post could be seen. Beyond the city, the Mount of Olives provided a background to the golden dome, rising above it to where the tall slim spire of the Russian Church stood like an arrow pointing heavenwards. In a corner of the balustraded roof where we were, a slim, bearded man in a long coat and wide-brimmed black hat was silently praying. He turned and greeted us, inviting Albert to join him. He explained in a gentle voice that he was a rabbi who lived quite a distance away and came every Sabbath Eve to this roof to pray facing the Temple site. His name was Uri.

Very soon Ya'acov, the first visitor to Ha-Ohel appeared, and with him a man and his two young sons. This little band had been coming regularly to the roof for Sabbath prayers. I joined them.

Flanking this roof was the tower of the Dormition Church where our soldiers were on constant guard behind the sand-bagged arches. On the roof of the small Franciscan Church just below us, two priests strolled back and forth in silent meditation.

The soldiers, attracted by our voices, watched respectfully. Some prayed with us without leaving their posts. Shadows of evening softened the gleam of the golden dome and enveloped the Old City. Before our prayers had ended, the voice of the muezzin was calling his Moslem brethren to worship, and church bells pealed out the hour of the Christian service.

Jerusalem, the centre of the world's main spiritual streams, was not only divided by military borders. I was convinced that one day the military barriers would be removed, and I believe that the spiritual barriers will also fall.

Our companions on the roof returned with us to Ha-Ohel. After reciting 'Kiddush'—the blessing on the wine, and joyously singing a Sabbath song, they hurriedly departed. We were the only ones then allowed to remain on Mount Zion after dark.

Early the next morning, the silence in Garden Square was filled with the blessings of Sabbath joy and peace. The day was different even for the pigeons: they had no need to wait for their food this morning, and were leisurely enjoying the remains of the double portion of food left for them by Obadiah on Friday.

In the little Sephardic synagogue, next to King David's Tomb, the worshippers arrived early. Their unrestrained Sabbath joy could be felt as their voices mingled in songs of prayer and thanksgiving.

The small congregation of the Ashkenazi synagogue above the Chamber of Destruction gathered a little later. Albert joined this handful of simple, devoted men who so strongly felt the holiness of Mount Zion in their hearts that they had walked great distances to satisfy their longing to worship on this Holy Hill.

C

A few women also came to pray here on the Sabbath. As I joined them in prayer, I was always deeply conscious that the atmosphere in this austere little synagogue, reclaimed from the ruins of Mount Zion, was imbued with a profounder measure of faith and devotion than I had found anywhere else. At the end of the service, in an ante-room, they pronounced the blessing on the wine and drank it with joy. Singing and dancing, the men concluded their Sabbath morning in the synagogue.

At dusk, Albert walked to the top of the Mount Zion steps and returned a little later with a very young soldier. The sabbath day was nearly ended.

I looked questioningly at Albert. 'This is Yehuda,' Albert introduced him. 'He is one of our neighbours from the military post and would like to share "Havdala" with us.'

The wine, candle and spices had already been prepared on the table for the Havdala service, the ceremony which terminates the Sabbath and marks the beginning of the new week. Yehuda's eyes lit up. 'It is like being at home with my parents,' he said.

I lighted the Havdala candle. The cup of wine was filled to overflowing and there were the sweet, scented spices. All spoke of health, happiness and blessing in the coming week. Albert read the prayer of thanksgiving for the distinction between light and darkness, between the holy and the profane. Then he recited the concluding prayer: '*Behold, God is my salvation; him will I trust, and not be afraid. For my strength and song is the Eternal and he hath been my succour. . . .*'

Thus the Sabbath ended and we wished each other 'shavua tov'—a good week.

*   *   *

With the end of the Sabbath, when the blessing of that day seems to linger on to welcome in the new week, a small band of orthodox worshippers assemble in the little Sephardic synagogue adjoining King David's Tomb, where, with

song and dance, they give praise and thanks for another
week.

As I watched, teenage boys with their well-curled side-
locks falling beneath their wide-brimmed black hats, accompanied their elder brothers and fathers, all carrying an
assortment of bags filled with food and drink. Plates and
glasses were set out on a long table, and salt herrings, bread,
nuts, cake and fruit were unpacked. Some of the men were
sitting reading prayers on benches facing the ark containing
the scrolls of the Law. The boys were in loud conversation
near by.

We were transported to another world as we observed
this scene through a small open door. Soon the benches
around the table were occupied. A long-bearded rabbi,
wearing a large fur-brimmed hat and a gold-and-black striped
caftan, sat at the head of the table. He broke off a piece of
bread, said the appropriate blessing, and then the meal
began.

The light from the old lamp hanging from the ceiling
seemed to diffuse its glow in a special way on this assembly
of men, old and young, gathered around the table in this
little synagogue, with its scrolls of the Law hidden behind
the red velvet curtains on which the Star of David was
embroidered in gold.

After they finished eating and had cleared up, a space was
made for dancing, for these Chasidic Jews believe in express-
ing their religious fervour in joyous dancing and singing. A
few onlookers had joined us outside the synagogue—other
religious Jews and curious visitors from other lands. When
those inside noticed us, we were warmly invited to join the
dancers. The men among us were led into the synagogue
itself, the women into a side room where we could watch.

With harmonium and drum as accompaniment the singing
and dancing soon began. All joined hands and danced in
circles. Unrestrained joy filled the little synagogue. Rabbis
and their children took the hands of their visitors, Jew

or Christian, Englishman or German alike. Together they
danced and sang, united in praise and thanksgiving. The
Light of Zion shone more brightly.

Our New Neighbours

It was not long after we had come to live on Mount Zion
that the sounds of workmen could be heard again from
within the thick stone walls of the ruined building behind
our house. David Palombo, the sculptor, had received permission to restore this building as a place in which to work
and exhibit his sculpture.

After many months of tireless effort, he transformed this
old ruin with its arched ceilings and thick pillars of stone,
into a most fitting setting for his work.

In Garden Square, facing the entrance to his gallery and
at the corner of our house, he erected one of his sculptures
which depicted wings. In his hands the cold, hard iron took
the form and grace of a vibrant wing. For me, this particular sculpture outside the entrance to Ha-Ohel was a per-
petual symbol of the unseen wings that I always felt to be
on Mount Zion, especially in times of difficulty and danger.

David Palombo and his young Chilean-born wife Yona
became our neighbours only during the day; at night we
were still alone.

However, new life was coming to Mount Zion. The
military authorities had decided to strengthen the border
guard and a group of ten young men on military service
was sent to Mount Zion. They were members of Nahal, a
unique branch of the Israeli army, whose young men and
women spend part of their military service farming by day
and doing guard duty by night. Most Nahal soldiers served
on the borders, where they established agricultural villages.

On Mount Zion it was different. The Nahal boys here
did guard duty and worked as printers. It was, in effect, an
urban Nahal outpost, and since this was Mount Zion all

the boys were from a religious school. They repaired a
house that stood right on the border and used it as their
living-quarters, and installed a small printing-press in a
room in a nearby building where they printed religious
literature.

On the Sabbath eve these religious Nahal soldiers helped
to make a 'minyan'—the congregation of ten men required
for a service in Jewish Law—on the roof above King
David's tomb, and Ha-Ohel became their second home.

The First Alarm

It was the end of the summer—when the land of Israel,
bathed in the sun for long months under a cloudless blue
canopy lies burnt and sear, crying out for water to quench
its thirst. With the onset of the winter rains, all nature seems
to echo King David's psalm: *'Sing unto the Lord with thanksgiving; sing praise upon the harp unto our God: who covereth the
heavens with clouds, who prepareth rain for the earth.'*

Work in the garden had to be suspended for the time.
The tourist season was over, and few people came to Mount
Zion. With the shortening days and the frequent storms of
lashing wind and heavy rain this danger zone held little
attraction for the visitor.

Only the very pious came to pray, among them Isaac and
his wife Bilha, for whom Mount Zion was the place nearest
to God. They spent many days living with us while their
new home was being built in Jerusalem.

It was while they were staying with us that we had an
unexpected call to go to Tel Aviv. We left Mount Zion on
the Wednesday, intending to be back in good time for the
Sabbath, but we were unavoidably detained until very early
on Sunday morning. There was a strange silence as we
lowered and relocked the barrier across the road up to
Mount Zion, and as Garden Square came into view we saw
that it was filled with groups of unfamiliar soldiers, guns,

and other military vehicles, which blocked the access to our house.

The soldiers, equally surprised at our appearance, asked: 'How did you get here? Don't you know that it is dangerous and nobody is being allowed up here today?'

Involved in family affairs, and with the Sabbath intervening, we had heard no news since Friday. We were now told that on Friday morning three of our soldiers on border patrol had been fired on by the Jordanians. An exchange of mortar and gunfire had lasted for some hours. Our military post on Mount Zion had been slightly damaged and bullets had reached into the City, but there had been no casualties.

The soldiers were emphatic: 'You cannot stay here.'

'We live here,' we explained to them, 'and have just returned from Tel Aviv. We knew nothing of what has been happening, but even if we had known we would still have come back.'

As we entered the house, we found Isaac and Bilha waiting with suitcases packed, their faces anxious.

'We're leaving,' Isaac said. 'We can't stay here another day. We wanted to leave earlier, but waited for your return. In any case, we were afraid to go out on the road yesterday.'

'It was terrible,' said Bilha. 'The house shook with the vibration of the big guns. The noise was deafening.' She trembled at the memory of it.

'When did all this happen?' I asked.

'Early Friday morning.'

'But it was all quiet after that, wasn't it?'

'Yes,' said Isaac, 'but we were afraid it would start again any moment. In fact Bilha was terrified.'

'Where did you kindle the Sabbath lights?' I asked.

'We were too afraid, we just sat in the corner under the stairs all the time until this morning.'

'Where will you go?' I asked as they prepared to leave.

'To Isaac's sister in Tel Aviv. It will be safer there,' replied Bilha.

As we began to arrange the day in this unexpected atmosphere, two of the young Nahal boys came to see us, accompanied by the commander of one of the new units posted on Mount Zion.

'The situation here is rather serious,' said the commander, 'and we do not like to have civilians around. We expect more trouble during the night or early morning and we advise you to go into the town and stay there until things have quietened down.'

'We would rather stay here,' I replied, and Albert agreed.

'But don't you realize the dangers?' he asked in surprise.

'We are always in danger,' I replied. 'After all there are dangers everywhere, and if this is our place, we do not like to leave it in times of danger. Perhaps we can be of some use if there is trouble, even if only to give you some coffee while you are waiting.' He smiled and walked away, shaking his head in disbelief.

Later, one of our Nahal boys came to me looking very troubled.

'What is it, Efraim?' I asked.

With heartfelt concern he pleaded with me: 'I feel about you as I would about my mother, if she were here,' he said. 'Please don't stay here tonight. I'll worry about you so much if the shooting starts again.'

I was deeply moved by his concern and even considered leaving for his sake: 'If your mother were here, Efraim,' I said, 'I don't think she'd want to leave if you were in danger; she'd surely prefer to stay near you.'

Efraim shook his head, and, after a moment of thoughtful silence, said: 'I'll tell my commander.'

A short time later, the commanding officer returned. 'We have decided to let you stay,' he said. 'But you mustn't go upstairs to your bedroom. Remain downstairs in the corner under the stairs. That's the safest place in this house. We may have to put a couple of soldiers in the loft.'

We agreed to do as he ordered. Nothing happened that night or the next day and after a few days the anxiety was over. Garden Square was again clear of troops and equipment, and life returned to normal. But the shadow of danger was always there, chilling and disquieting, even on the warmest and most peaceful of days.

The First Hanukka

Winter enveloped Mount Zion in a cold, dark, wet mantle: the days were short and silent, the nights long and dark. In this season, Hanukka—the Festival of Light—is celebrated.

While nobody was allowed to come to Mount Zion at night, we often had visitors staying with us overnight. Among them at that time was Ya'acov, the pockets of whose shapeless garments always bulged with Bibles.

On this first eve of Hanukka that we celebrated on Mount Zion, he and our family of Nahal boys gathered around the table in the warmth and intimacy of our kitchen corner. Outside a gale swept the Mount, driving beating rain against the windows with such force and noise that we thought they would break or blow open at any moment. But we felt as peaceful and secure as if we had been enclosed in a magic shell of protection.

The feast of Hanukka commemorates the stirring deeds of the Maccabees, a small band of courageous men who refused to worship pagan idols and, rising up in revolt, cleansed the desecrated Temple in Jerusalem. On entering the Sanctuary they found a single cruse of oil, the contents sufficient to last for a day. But the Temple was illuminated for eight days until a new supply of oil could be obtained.

The 'menorah'—the eight-branched candlestick lit in remembrance of this miracle—stood on our table. A new candle would be lit on each of the eight nights of the feast.

We kindled the first Hanukka light with its appropriate prayer. Then we chanted the hymn: '*O Fortress, Rock of my salvation, unto thee it is becoming to give praise: let my house of prayer be restored.*'

For us, sitting so close to the Temple area, then in enemy hands, these words had a special added significance. We were reminded of the constant attempts that had been made to destroy the Jews and of the miracles of God's deliverances. Now again we were surrounded by the enemy, threatening us with extermination, planning to drive us into the sea. The enemy camps were all around us.

Ya'acov opened one of his well-worn Bibles and read to us from Isaiah: '*Behold the Lord's hand is not shortened that it cannot save: neither his ear heavy that it cannot hear.*'

The first little Hanukka candle seemed to burn with an extra brightness. The boys sang cheerfully while I heated oil in a large frying-pan and dropped into it the 'latkes'— potato fritters—the food traditionally eaten on this festival. Hot and golden brown straight from pan to plate, they were eaten with much relish. I seemed to be making them endlessly. . . .

It was also the birthday of our little terrier Tamar, and there was a birthday cake in her honour. The soldiers sang birthday songs for her as she danced round the room on her hind legs.

The Nahal boys finally departed, taking with them a dish of latkes for the soldiers on duty at the military post. They went out into the darkness with the cold wind driving the rain into their faces. I closed and locked the door on the stormy night, wondering what lay in store for these boys, what tests they would have to pass to prove their courage and faith.

I returned upstairs to our kitchen, Ya'acov was still reading the Bible.

'How long do you think it'll be, Ya'acov,' I asked, 'before we have peace in Israel and Jerusalem is no longer divided?'

'As long as the Creator wills,' he replied and, opening another small Bible, read from the Psalms: *'Great is the Lord, and greatly to be praised in the city of our God, in the mountains of his holiness.'*

Visitors

We did not remain alone for long. Two Christian friends, Jack and Mildred, came from South Africa to spend a month with us on Mount Zion. Their dream of coming to Jerusalem had been realized after years of working, saving and planning.

At the same time, Joseph, a relative from the States, was also staying with us for a short while. He, an artist and musician, was also realizing a long-cherished ambition to roam the world.

Joseph was returning late one afternoon after wandering around Mount Zion. I met him in Garden Square and we sat for a while on a bench facing the Chamber of Destruction. The caretaker, at the door, was calling someone inside to hurry. A long-bearded, long-coated elderly man emerged —the Rabbi. He had just concluded his prayers. The caretaker hastily locked the door after him.

'Shalom! Shalom!' they called as they hurried away, anxious to leave Mount Zion while there was still daylight.

'It is like being in another world, up here,' Joseph said.

'What do you find so different?' I asked.

'Everything here directs my thoughts into unaccustomed channels—thoughts of religion, of Jewishness,' he replied. 'I'd never given much thought to religion,' he went on. 'My violin and my paintings have helped me through many hard knocks in my life and have given me much joy and satisfaction. I see religion in the beauty of life,' he said, 'and in trying to express what I feel about it, I find fulfilment.

I see God in flowers, the sunset, the colours and contours of Nature.'

'Surely God is in everything,' I replied. 'Do you find Him only in the beauties of Nature?'

'I don't understand the meaning of life or death or the way mankind has filled the earth with evil and destruction since time immemorial. There are good fellows and bad fellows: I go my own way, but I suppose I try as far as possible to join the good fellows, and try not to harm my fellow-men.'

Joseph seemed to be speaking as much to himself as to me as he continued: 'All the complications of thought I leave to philosophers, psychologists and sages. All the unsolved problems of life and death I leave to the religious mystics whatever their creed, and there are plenty of them in the world, each offering his own explanation.'

The shadows deepened and it was beginning to get cold. I did not want to intrude my own thoughts, and we walked back to the house in silence.

On the next Sabbath eve, Joseph, Albert and Ya'acov returned from the service on the roof. We sat around the table on which stood the two lighted Sabbath candles, the wine waiting to be poured into the glasses and the two Sabbath loaves—'chalot'—under their cover, waiting for the blessing. It was with a deep feeling of Sabbath peace and thanksgiving that we partook of the meal.

It was then we heard sounds which made us look enquiringly at one another. Had shots been fired? Listening more closely we heard machine-guns being fired somewhere close by—'tack, tack, tack . . .'

'Somebody is having a game,' said Albert cheerfully, trying to allay the anxiety in everyone's eyes.

It was soon quiet again and it was only the next day that our curiosity was satisfied. We heard that our Arab neighbours had shot some of their own people who had been condemned to death. It might have been otherwise.

After the meal, Ya'acov sang some 'zmeroth'—Sabbath songs—in his deep melodious voice: '*The Sabbath brings God's gift of vigour, to give thee courage to seek his face . . .*'

Later, as Joseph listened to Ya'acov expounding the Bible, finding in it an answer to every problem and a guide for every step, memories long buried within him came to life. He told us: 'My parents came to New York from a "shtetl"—a small village—in Poland. I can still remember my father chanting the morning prayers before going out to the menial work which provided his family with a living.'

Joseph's eyes seemed a little misty as he recalled those early days as immigrants: 'My father always spoke of his longing to come to Jerusalem, his desire to be buried in the Holy Land. Needless to say, he was buried in Brooklyn,' he added parenthetically.

'And here you are, his son, with us now in Jerusalem,' Albert interjected.

'Not only in Jerusalem, but on Mount Zion, which my father, and all the others like him, regarded as a very sacred place.'

Joseph was silent a while, before continuing his story: 'After my barmitzvah, I also put on tefillin—phylacteries— each morning and said prayers regularly. I was happy when I prayed.'

He told us how the time had come for him to go to college. There nobody had prayed, and he had felt too embarrassed to do so. 'I did not want to be different from the other boys. I gave it up.' After his parents died, he felt as though his Jewish roots had been stifled. He sometimes forgot that he was a Jew. 'Israel,' he said, 'was to have been just another one of the stops on my world tour, but now that I am here, something seems to be happening to me.'

'You have come home,' I said, for I believed that his dormant roots were taking nourishment from the original soil in which Judaism had been planted. The impact of some

of the Judaic symbols was awakening in him once again the
consciousness of belonging to the Jewish family.

He sat there looking thoughtful and then turning to Jack,
he asked: 'What brought you to Israel? How do you feel
in this Jewish atmosphere? Isn't it very strange for you?'

Jack and Mildred had listened attentively to all the
prayers and songs, as I kindled the Sabbath candles, and I
had sensed the deep reverence within them. 'We are in
Israel,' replied Jack, 'because we believe that all we have
has spiritually come to us through the Jews and that the
redemption of the world will come through Israel.'

Joseph listened with great interest as Jack continued: 'My
mother, a very devout Christian, was considered a rebel by
her family and her community. She left the church because
she claimed it had lost its vision and had been the cause of
so much Jewish persecution. She taught us, as children, to
love the Jews, to remember always that Jesus was a Jew
and that we had received our Christian faith through the
Jews. She believed that it was only in repentance for the
sins committed against the Jews that we could receive the
blessings of Zion.'

'She sounds a very unusual woman,' I said.

'That she certainly was,' Jack replied. 'You know, she
died before the State of Israel was proclaimed, but she
always taught us that the independence of Israel would be
a sign for great rejoicing. It meant that we would be approaching the time when the Jewish people would be able
to fulfil their mission.'

'Mission!' Joseph echoed. '—Would you like to explain
that to me?'

'Of course! My mother believed that the Jews had been
called into being as a nation through which God could show
His power and His glory. With them He would inaugurate
His Kingdom on earth, a Kingdom of peace for all creation.'

'And when do you think that will be?' asked Joseph.

'The establishment of the State of Israel is, we believe, a

step towards the Kingdom of Israel. Not the political kingdom which the enemies of Israel accuse the Jews of striving
for, but the Kingdom of God on earth, with the Messiah
as ruler and His throne on Mount Zion.'

Mildred nodded agreement and added: 'Because we believe
this you must know how privileged we feel to be here now
on Mount Zion with our Jewish friends, and to have shared
this Sabbath eve with you all.'

Joseph looked a little puzzled—he had never heard
Christians expounding such views before. But Ya'acov,
undeterred, opened a Bible and read from Isaiah: '*For the
Lord will have mercy on Jacob, and will yet choose Israel and set
them in their own land: and the strangers shall be joined with them,
and they shall cleave to the house of Jacob.*'

When Joseph left us some days later with violin, paints
and canvases strapped to his back, his departing words were:
'The spirit of Mount Zion came over me during the time
spent with you all in this house. I think I will see Jerusalem
through different eyes now. These days here on Mount Zion
have unlocked a corner of my heart which I did not believe
existed any longer.'

*   *   *

It was becoming known in different circles in Jerusalem and
elsewhere that we were living on Mount Zion. People
responded at first with incredulity.

We began to have frequent visitors. Some came out of
curiosity, others because of a deep interest, and some
because of a strong religious feeling and reverence for this
Holy Hill. Because of the location of Ha-Ohel conversation
invariably turned to the Bible, its references to or promises
for Mount Zion. Or it turned to the contemplation of our
faith—the faith which dispelled any fears of living here.

All who came to this house, believers and non-believers,
Jews and Christians alike, seemed to experience the peace
and blessing promised for Mount Zion. One guest of little

faith said on leaving: 'Coming here is really like coming to a haven of peace. Guns at the ready on one side, and the hustle and bustle of the City on the other have not impaired the atmosphere of peace and serenity. May it be for all time.'

Early one morning the door bell rang. I looked through the window and saw, standing at the gate, a young man with a light brown beard, side-curls and clear grey eyes. He wore the costume of the orthodox—a traditional long satin coat and a wide mink-trimmed hat. He introduced himself as I opened the gate for him: 'I am Rabbi Twilensky. I have heard that someone has come to live on Mount Zion. Is this the house?'

He spoke in Yiddish, the language of Mea Shearim, the orthodox quarter of Jerusalem, where Hebrew is the language of the Bible and not for daily use.

'Come in and meet my husband,' I said as he entered. He stood silently gazing for some moments through the door opening out on to the balcony, his slight, long-coated figure silhouetted against the sky. He seemed to be looking into eternity. Then he turned and grasped Albert's hand. His whole being radiated warmth.

'Now that you have come to live here,' he said to Albert, 'the Messiah will surely soon be coming.' He embraced Albert, and with great restraint refrained from embracing me.

'If you both had faith enough to come and live here in this time of danger it shows the beginning of the restoration of King David's throne on Mount Zion. Your prayers will be answered and your faith will prepare the way for the coming of the Messiah, for the Kingdom of God on earth.'

Rabbi Twilensky became a frequent visitor to Ha-Ohel. His thanksgiving was always expressed in song and dance. On many a Sabbath when he visited us, drooping spirits were raised from despair to hope, from anxiety to joy, by the songs and stories which sprang spontaneously from his simple faith.

'We must be better Jews,' he was always saying. 'All Jews must be obedient to the Torah—and then the Messiah will come.'

When we visited his home in Mea Shearim some time later to meet his wife and five young children, we were shocked by the conditions in which they lived. They had one room, one wall of which was green with damp. But the children clamoured around us with happy faces, their mother trying her best to keep them in order. There was no sadness, no complaints.

When I spoke to Rabbi Twilensky about his position, he replied: 'This is the home our Father has given us. We are thankful to him for it.'

'Is your Father also in Mea Shearim?' I asked.

'Of course,' he replied. 'My Father lives everywhere and knows everything. We thank Him for the blessing of our children and when our Father thinks we should have a better home, He will give it to us.'

I was silenced.

The Garden

The first steps were being taken to prepare for our garden. The stones around the house were carefully sorted and put aside for rebuilding the wall; the mulberry trees and an olive tree were freed of their surrounding rubble and their twisted branches were trimmed and supported.

There was no soil, just the dust and stone of the hilltop which we carried off in lorry loads, and replaced with topsoil brought from another sacred site—the Tombs of the Sanhedrim—where excavation was being done. A layer of this soil a metre deep soon covered the grey rubble and made the base of our garden to be.

The Jordanian soldiers watched these activities, hands on their guns. To them it must have looked as if military fortifications were being strengthened. They would never have believed that a garden was being made under their very eyes.

While the rains and the intermittent days of sunshine were doing their part in preparing the soil for planting, I began to plan the garden in my mind thinking of the plants and trees I would put into it. At that time there were very few gardens in Jerusalem; and those had only geraniums and hardy flowering shrubs, and in some rare corners, roses.

I was told that it would be hard to find anyone with a real knowledge of gardening. The people of Israel had had to meet so many more urgent demands, the building up of the State, the absorption of the new immigrants from seventy-four countries, and with all the accompanying problems, there had been no time then to think of anything like gardens. But this vision I had of a garden on Mount Zion had a special meaning and I felt it was a task I had to fulfil.

How would I plan the garden? What would I plant? Where would I find the plants? Who would help me with the hard work at the beginning? I remembered the sub-tropical gardens I had loved in South Africa: the beautiful lilies, the red and white amaryllis, the blue clusters of agapanthus, the pink and gold tiger lilies, the lovely patterned leaves, and the scarlet hibiscus flowers opening their petals wide like little flares of light on their green outspread branches. I remembered the profusion of bougain-villea flowers in red, purple and gold. And then the jaca-randa trees—their bouquets of blue-mauve, bell-shaped flowers resting on delicate ferny foliage, like blue mist floating through the branches. I thought of the incredibly beautiful strelitzia, the exotic 'Bird of Paradise' flower.

Many of these flowers I had seen also in Israel—mostly along the coastal plain: even jacaranda trees near Tel Aviv.

Then I remembered the gardens of England, awakening in spring after the long, frosty winter—crocuses, hyacinths, daffodils, tulips, irises, narcissi; then later the many-coloured

D

herbaceous borders, where the delphiniums, in different
shades of blue, were my favourite.

In my dream garden I saw all these things growing
together on this barren and stony Mount Zion. I wondered
if it would be possible—but so much that had seemed impossible had already proved otherwise. Perhaps this dream
would also be realized.

At this time I found Simon, the one professional gardener
in Jerusalem, who sometimes helped out on archaeological
digs as there was not always enough gardening work in
Jerusalem to keep him busy.

I thought the entrance pathway to the house would have
to be higher than the garden and built along the side of an
old wild orange tree we had found half-buried in the rubble.
A winding stone path with steps would lead down into the
lower secluded area, enclosed within the rebuilt garden
walls. This path would curve around a little area under the
mulberry trees, where I planned to plant a lawn. Between
it and the wall would be fruit trees and flowers, with one
corner set aside for roses.

When I described the path to the workmen they insisted
that it could only be built straight. 'Why curves?' they had
asked—'the stones are meant to be straight.' In the end,
ignoring their laughter, I placed each stone myself, creating
the pattern I had in my mind.

The garden was now ready for planting, and I began my
search for the plants I wanted. Not much was to be found
in Jerusalem. Simon had explained that high and exposed
as we were to the violent winter winds, and the hot desert
sandstorms of summer, hardly anything would grow.

I listened to his advice, and thought it wiser at this stage
not to tell him of the things I intended to put into this
garden, if only I could find them.

From a friend in Holland I received bulbs of all the
spring flowers I remembered in my English garden. I went
all over the country—Tel Aviv, Haifa, Galilee, in search of

plants and I collected a variety of roses, lilies, oleander and hibiscus plants. I found young saplings of peach, plum, apple, almond, pomegranate, loquat, lemon, and vines. One day I returned home with some gerbera plants and to my great joy I even found a young jacaranda tree. 7 4-/9 6

The soil, richly fed, was now ready to receive and nourish these tender young plants. I put each one into the open soil with the prayer that it would grow and blossom in praise of the Lord of Heaven and Earth, and that it would bring joy and healing to this corner of Mount Zion.

Simon, when he saw them, was outraged and said scornfully: 'You're wasting your time and money with these plants. They'll never grow in Jerusalem, especially not on this exposed, stony hill. They need the humid heat and sandy soil of the coastal plain.'

'Everything will grow here,' I replied.

Simon, who had faith only in the work of his hands, looked upon me as one who had never grown up or had much contact with the reality of life as he knew it.

I smiled at him and said: 'Let's wait and see what happens.'

We dug a deep, deep hole at the corner near the front of the house, where the steps curved down into the lower garden, removed more of the grey dust and replaced it with good soil and manure. As we lowered the root of the little Jacaranda tree into its new home, Simon's scepticism could not quench my faith. There would be an answer to my prayer for a blessing on this sapling, which held mysteriously within itself the promise of future beauty.

Working in a garden, in contact with the earth and the elements of Nature, gives me a deeper consciousness of the power which governs and is the source of all life. It makes me realize my dependence upon that power, and at the same time gives me the feeling of working together with God. It is the divine spark in the soul of man which unites him with the divine power and calls upon him to do his share in the partnership—to understand and minister to the needs of divine creation in whatever form it is manifested: plant, animal and, above all, human.

As the roots of each little plant were enclosed in the earth I knew that if I did not care for them by giving water when they were thirsty, air when stifled, shade or sun as needed, they would die or else be stunted in their growth. As I chose the places in the garden for the different plants, according to their needs, Simon seemed surprised at my knowledge.

'Where did you study gardening?' he asked.

'Almost all I know I have learned from the plants themselves. I've always had a little garden—and when I didn't know what to do I watched the plants and their response to my treatment. In this way I learned what was best for them. I asked the Creator to give me the necessary understanding.'

Simon grinned: 'I suppose the Creator has an agricultural school up there,' he said, pointing to the sky. 'He must have some very good teachers.'

'Love is the teacher, Simon,' I said, ignoring his cynicism, 'love teaches us all we need to know. When men seek to learn by love how to deal with all problems, not only of plant life but of human life, we'll have found the solution to most of our troubles and a world where "*they shall beat their swords into plowshares . . . But they shall sit every man under his vine and under his fig tree; and none shall make them afraid*".'

Simon looked in the direction of the Jordanian military post facing us. The heads of the Arab soldiers could be seen above the sandbags.

'Talk to *them* about love,' he answered, 'and you'll get a few bullets to silence you.'

'Yes, Simon, love is not *yet* the ruling power in the hearts of men. Therefore, there are wars and bullets and suffering and fear, but the time will come when that will be changed and the prophecy I quoted from Isaiah will be realized. I believe that the prophecies are the promises of the Almighty and that those promises will be fulfilled.'

Simon shrugged his shoulders and dug his fork into the earth: 'Give me facts, not promises,' he said. 'If you can believe those promises, it must make life easy for you.'

'Not easy,' I replied, 'but worth while.'

Memories of the Holocaust

Ilana, a relative from South Africa, arrived to spend some days with us on Mount Zion. The happy reunion revived memories of our first meeting in 1945, when after a long search among the survivors of concentration camps in Germany her brother had found her alive and had brought her to our home in London. She was then a young woman of twenty who, separated from her family in Poland, had lived through all the hardships of the Warsaw Ghetto, the horrors of the death camps and had endured the final march. . . .

'How often I prayed for death to deliver me,' she told us when we first met her. 'But each time death held out its liberating hand I was snatched back by life, to continue as prisoner in a hell on earth.'

Slowly she regained health and strength, and went out to her relatives in South Africa. A good husband and three lovely children have brought her happiness, but her experiences have left their ineradicable mark.

Now she was on Mount Zion. As she stood on the balcony of Ha-Ohel, looking at the scene which opened out before her, tears filled her eyes: 'Am I not a very privileged woman?' she repeatedly asked. 'My life was spared by miracles so that I could be on Mount Zion. Six million Jews perished but I was saved to come to this holy place. Why me? This miracle has made me the happiest woman in the world today.'

The following day we made our way to the basement of the Ashkenazi synagogue, one of the most hallowed places on Mount Zion. Here was the Vault of Catastrophe, also known as the Chamber of Martyrs, dedicated to the memory of the six million who had perished.

Dimly lit arched rooms and alcoves contain the grim reminders of the Holocaust. The stone walls are covered with plaques bearing the names of whole communities, large and small, the members of which perished in Nazi concentration camps. In showcases are the remains of desecrated Torah Scrolls, blood-stained and torn prayer shawls among other articles. One alcove has a model of a part of the wall in the Warsaw ghetto behind which courageous Jews had risen against their enemy in an attempt doomed to failure.

The memories of those bitter days welled up again as Ilana recognized the exhibit. She told us how she had been with her best friends Ben and Sarah in those last, dark days in the Ghetto. Both were to be in the forefront of the resistance planned for the next day. They were conscious of the odds against them, and a sense of foreboding was strong within them.

Their frantic concern was for their five-year-old son Ari, who they knew would sooner or later fall into the hands of the Nazis. They had finally agreed to put an end to his life. But Ari did not die so easily, and Ilana, who had remained with him, had coaxed the flickering flame of life back into him.

'Some weeks later,' Ilana continued, 'they allowed me to carry the frail and weakened Ari into the trucks taking us to the gas chambers. But on arrival at our destination, he was wrenched screaming from my arms, and I never saw him again.'

She had been left standing in the long lines destined for the gas chamber when at the last moment they had called her to join the line of those to whom work was being allocated. 'The gas chamber was too easy.'

We stood for a while before a slightly raised platform of black stone. On it was a lamp from which rose the eternal flame—symbol of eternal life—and around its base were inscribed the names of the concentration camps, the twentieth-century roll call of man's inhumanity to man: Bergen-Belsen, Dachau, Auschwitz, Treblinka . . .

Slowly and silently, we walked into the small vaulted recess where black-and-white striped urns contain the ashes of some of the six million. Above them were exhibits of soap made from human fat and cylinders of Cyclone B gas, used in the attempt to exterminate the Jews.

Ilana stood before these ashes motionless, tearless, her body rigid, her face frozen. Almost inaudible was the cry she emitted: 'Ben, Sara, Ari . . . all my companions of those years . . . we meet again here.' Then her lips framed the words written on the wall beside the exhibits: 'I believe with absolute faith in the resurrection of the dead. I believe with absolute faith that the Messiah will come, and even though he tarry, I will wait for him every day.'

These selfsame words, 'I believe . . . (Ani ma'amin) . . .' had been on the lips of the Jews entering the gas chambers.

The Rabbi who sat daily in the Chamber of the Martyrs and whose task it was to say the prayers for the departed souls, gave Ilana a candle. She lit it with a silent prayer and placed it before the ashes of the victims of the Holocaust.

We turned and looked at the six little alcoves in the wall, representing the six concentration camp ovens, filled with the burnt-out candles which had been lit in memory of the dead. Then we paused again for a few moments before the eternal flame and walked out into the little courtyard, lined with more plaques inscribed with the names of lost communities. An obelisk stands there in memory of the children who were so cruelly murdered. Unceasing drops of water trickle down its sides, symbolizing the tears of the mothers of Israel.

The words of Jeremiah kept running through my head: '*A voice was heard in Ramah, lamentation and bitter weeping;*

Rachel weeping for her children refused to be comforted for her children, because they were not.'

'The hardest trial of all,' said Ilana in tears, 'was to see the children, babies, torn from their mothers' arms thrown to the gas chamber.'

Suddenly we heard the voices of children, happy voices, uninhibited voices—the voice of a free Israel. A group of school children and their teacher were being shown the holy places of Mount Zion. Here they would learn something of Israel's history, her destiny, her as yet unrealized hopes.

It suddenly seemed to me as if Jeremiah were standing with us: *'Thus saith the Lord; Refrain thy voice from weeping, and thine eyes from tears: for thy work shall be rewarded, saith the Lord; and they shall come again from the land of the enemy. And there is hope in thine end, saith the Lord, that thy children shall come again to their own border.'*

Then we were out again in the sunlight, the birds joyously acclaiming the approach of spring, the air scented with its breath, and Ilana asked: 'How? How could God have allowed such things to happen to our people?'

'Perhaps the answer is in our Daily Prayer Book,' I said. 'The Rock, perfect in every work, who can say unto him, What workest thou? He ruleth below and above: he causeth death and revivest. The Rock, perfect in every deed, who can say unto him, What doest thou?'

'But anti-Semitism is still strong in the world,' said Ilana shaking her head. 'All that happened in Germany hasn't changed the hatred for the Jews. Now Egypt's Nasser continues with the same aim as Hitler. Have we really any real friends among the nations?'

'Anti-Semitism will continue,' I replied, 'until the spirit of the Messiah rules in the world.'

Ilana and I walked slowly across Garden Square and entered our garden. The rose bushes were beginning to hide their nakedness under the first unfolding leaf buds. The tiny seedlings which I had planted some weeks earlier were standing sturdy and confident, their roots firmly established in the earth, their green leaves spreading in response to the directing rays of the sun. Strong green spearheads pushed through the earth, announcing the life surge of daffodils, tulips, hyacinths, and other bulbs hidden below. The grass seeds sown under the mulberry trees had produced a shimmer of pale green, soft and tender as the hair of a baby's head.

We sat on a bench under the mulberry trees, contemplating all these wonders of Nature.

'Look,' I said, 'you cannot quench life. It rises triumphant from the grave.'

*   *   *

I thought of Ilana a few months later as workmen were finishing the task of erecting a stone monument at the entrance to the Chamber of Destruction, a replica of the wooden monument over the mass graves of Bergen-Belsen.

At the dedication ceremony a few days later, a little group of people stood around this draped monument, survivors and relatives of the victims of the concentration camps. They stood motionless as the prayers for the dead were recited. Their eyes were dry as though the fountain of tears had been drained.

A former Brigadier of the British Army had come especially to be present at this ceremony. He had been among the first to liberate Bergen-Belsen. His eyes were fixed on the stone on which was engraved: 'Earth conceal not the blood shed on thee'. It was not the stone he saw, but the earth still wet with the blood that had been spilt. Beside him stood those whose dear ones had been drenched in that blood.

In the silence which followed the prayers only the fluttering of wings could be heard—the pigeons on Mount Zion. Or was it the echo of celestial wings?

Chapter Three

It was spring. Nature had unlocked the doors of its hidden workshop and life surged upwards, responding to the warm welcome of the sun. It was the season of the first great Jewish Festival of the year—Pesach (Passover)—the festival of deliverance.

The birds were busy preparing their nests; flower buds were tinted overnight in a medley of colours. Jewish housewives were cleaning out their cupboards and ordering their supply of matzot—unleavened bread.

The Festival of Pesach

Now it was the eve of Pesach. In every Jewish home in Israel, the 'seder' was being prepared. Families were gathered together to read the Haggadah, the story of the Exodus from Egypt, and to rejoice in our present freedom.

Nobody was to be seen on Mount Zion. There was a stillness in which even Nature seemed to be holding her breath. Only the soldiers on guard duty were at their posts. Most of the others had been given leave to spend the evening with their families. There was a festive atmosphere in Ha-Ohel, and many happy voices could be heard. Friends from different countries had come to celebrate this—our first seder on Mount Zion—with us.

The garden had triumphantly fulfilled its promise and the rooms were filled with its flowers. On the festive table stood the lighted candles, the plate with the traditional symbols: the roasted shankbone to commemorate the pascal sacrifice which our ancestors brought to the Temple on

Pesach in ancient times; bitter herbs as a reminder of Israel's bondage in Egypt: 'haroshet', a mixture of grated apple, dates, nuts, cinnamon and wine, symbolizing the mortar which the Israelites had used in building for Pharaoh, its sweetness also a sign of hope for freedom; a roasted egg, the traditional symbol of sacrifice. On another plate were the matzot, and in the centre of the table stood Elijah's cup. It is believed that the prophet Elijah, the messenger of God, appointed to herald the era of the Messiah, comes to every home to sip the seder wine.

Eighteen people shared the festival with us. They had come from England, America, South Africa, Germany and Israel—and were both Jews and Christians. This seder on Mount Zion was the fulfilment of a dream for people of both religions who had 'joined themselves to the House of Jacob'.

During the service we all experienced a deep sense of awe. Subsequently one of our guests remarked that only a few yards from this house was the room in which, according to tradition, Jesus and his disciples celebrated their seder or 'last supper' nearly two thousand years ago. Another pointed out, however, that after that occasion the Temple had been destroyed.

In summing up the discussion that followed I asked: 'But now that we have a "first seder" again on Mount Zion, can we not hope that soon the Temple will be rebuilt?'

*　　*　　*

Two days later hundreds of people walked below our window. It was the day of the great annual Passover pilgrimage to Mount Zion. A colourful human stream flowed slowly down the road, which was lined with the blue and white banners of the State of Israel, and into the valley from where the steps leading to Mount Zion begin.

There, like a multi-coloured ribbon drawn by invisible hands, it mounted the winding stone steps, rising higher and higher until it reached the summit.

Jewish communities from the Arab lands were led by their rabbis and elders, who wore flowing robes and brightly and beautifully coloured headgear. Under gold-fringed canopies the Torah Scrolls were carried, their decorative silver casings gleaming where the sun's rays caught them. Bearded Chasidim and other orthodox groups in their gold-and-black-striped caftans and fur-trimmed hats, sang joyously as they hugged their Torah Scrolls.

At the head of the steps, hoisted on twelve high flagpoles, the standards bearing the emblems of the twelve tribes of Israel were gently moving in the breeze. Beneath them, a large crowd of sightseers had been gathering since the early morning, to await the arrival of the pilgrims.

The leaders of the procession were mounting the last steps, and behind them came their unending stream of followers. They pushed their way through the sightseers, entering the dark vaulted chambers of the old stone building, crossed the small sunlit courtyard and entered the room which led to the place hallowed as the Tomb of David. Here, through a wrought-iron gate, can be seen the large stone sarcophagus covered with red velvet, embroidered in gold. On it stand a number of crowns, one for each year of Israel's independence.

The dense crowd, some praying, some singing, some in silent meditation, others giving ecstatic cries, was jostled past the Tomb. I overheard an English tourist saying to a friend: 'This is like a frenzied cult of idol worship!'

I looked into the tear-filled eyes of an old Yemenite, who seemed unaware of the noisy, pushing crowds around him. His lips were moving in silent prayer. Was he thanking God for his deliverance, for his return to the Promised Land? Was he communing with King David, praying that the son of David, the Messiah, would soon come to reign on this throne? Was he already feeling His presence on this Holy Mount?

Life on Mount Zion

In the stillness of the night, every sound has a special significance. The night sounds on Mount Zion conjured up pictures. I could see soldiers, guns, enemies, marauders, wild dogs, jackals. To all these familiar sounds a new sound was now added—a baby's cry!

David Palombo, the sculptor, was working day and night to finish the gates he had been commissioned to make for the Knesset (Parliament) in time for its opening. For this reason he had finally been given permission to live above his gallery. He, Yona, his wife, and their month-old daughter Paulita became our close neighbours. The entrance to the Palombo gallery from Garden Square was practically on our back doorstep.

Yona, small and slim, with thick, silky black hair, olive skin and shining grey eyes, had been Palombo's student. Creative herself, she was now his assistant. She was fearless, and while pregnant had driven their jeep up and down the mountain under the watchful eyes of Arab and Israeli soldiers.

Now the Palombos were busy repairing a large ruined room above the Gallery. Walls, windows and roof were reconstructed to make it habitable and soon it was transformed into living-room, bedroom and kitchen, all in one. All were artistic expressions of David and Yona. The seasoned wood of a large tree-trunk worked with a mosaic top served as a table. A beautiful mosaic screen separated the kitchen corner, and sculptured iron utensils and lamps hung on the walls. Paulita's little cot in the far corner gave the warm human touch of family life.

The room opened out on to a spacious flat roof and there were more derelict rooms leading off it. Later this became a roof garden, a haven for Paulita, and the other rooms were restored and used as workrooms.

*　　*　　*

We were a very strange assortment of souls gathered on Mount Zion and had come from many lands. The outdoor workers and the pious men who worked in the offices of the administrative body were from Morocco, Iraq, Tunisia, Turkey, Yemen, South America and also West Europe. They, together with the Nahal boys, the soldiers and the priests of the Dormition and Franciscan Churches, made up the 'family' of Mount Zion.

Ha-Ohel welcomed them all. The extreme differences in culture, background, temperament and character seemed to dissolve and melt away in this atmosphere of peace, faith and friendliness. However diverse our thoughts and ways, one deep bond seemed to unite us all—faith in the God of Israel, reverence for this holy Mount and belief in the promises for its future. Our lives were like threads woven into the pattern of Mount Zion.

One morning, looking out of my window, I saw a little band of the simple oriental workers gathered around a beautiful white donkey. They were very excited. I went down to them, and was told that this animal had strayed over the border from Jordan and had joined the donkeys of Mount Zion which were used for transporting loads up the steps Nobody had succeeded in driving it back across the border, and there was a very lively discussion going on about it. I saw one old man praying emotionally.

'Now the Messiah will surely come,' exclaimed one of the men, 'for has not this beautiful white donkey come here to await him?'

Their work seemed to be much lighter for them that day. And the white donkey remained on Mount Zion.

One of the workers, a bent little old man with a long reddish beard, was responsible for taking the rubbish of Mount Zion to be burned near the iron fence at the border. I saw him still sitting there one day long after the rubbish had burned away, and I went down to see if he was feeling all right.

Leaning with his back against the fence, on the other side of which were the Arab soldiers, he was far away in another world—busy writing poetry. A survivor of the concentration camps, he was writing praises of the Almighty for his deliverance.

*   *   *

The peace and quiet of Mount Zion was little disturbed by the sound of traffic. Military vehicles travelled on the road, mostly at night. During the day there was an occasional army car, or the Palombo's jeep or scooter to which we had already become accustomed.

Each morning, David would go down in his jeep to bring up his assistants and any materials he required. The noise of his scooter, on which he rushed to and from the city, was equally part of our daily life. Any other unfamiliar sounds drew us to the window to see what strange car had been allowed on the road.

Sometimes it was the car from the Ministry of Religion, bringing Dr Kahane, the Curator of Mount Zion. But one day a very large van came noisily up the road. Curious, we went out to see why the military barrier across the road had been raised for this transport. It stopped at the small door to the passageway, leading to King David's Tomb. The door of the van was opened and very carefully and tenderly ten wheelchairs and their occupants were lifted out. There were ten young boys, their crippled legs hanging limply or in iron supports—victims of polio.

They had reached their thirteenth birthday and this visit to Mount Zion was to celebrate their Bar Mitzvah, an important day for each one of them, the day when the Jewish boy reads a portion of the Law in the synagogue and takes on the responsibility of being a Jew.

The chairs were lifted up the few steps to the entrance and the boys wheeled themselves through the dark chamber where memorial candles were flickering, to the room beside

King David's Tomb, sometimes used for prayer. There they
were met by parents and relatives, rabbis and other members
of the Mount Zion 'family', waiting for the ceremony to
begin.

In the sad, pale faces of the boys, some eyes were shining,
others were clouded. This was a special occasion for these
boys, debarred from normal life. They wrapped their prayer
shawls around their shoulders, wound their phylactories
around their left arms and on their heads. Then each boy,
sitting in his wheelchair, read his portion of the Torah.

*   *   *

There were days when nobody was allowed on Mount Zion
—not even the workers, because of border incidents. Days
when the only voice to be heard was the chant of the
muezzin from the minaret near by, calling the Moslems to
prayer.

On one of these silent days I was working in the garden
and was surprised to hear a voice calling to me. Simon, the
gardener, who had helped me in the initial stages of the
garden, had managed to come through with a soldier friend
who was also a gardener. He had not been here for five
months.

We walked around the garden and looked at the flowers
which blossomed profusely in every corner, the young fruit
trees and shrubs also showed vigorous growth.

Tender green vine leaves were making delicate patterns
on a part of the old stone walls of the house; white-flecked
variegated ivy was racing upwards along another wall. Calla
lilies unfolded their white sheaths to reveal the golden
stamen rods within. The paths were lined with sweet white
alyssum curving in a lacy border along the edge of the
stones. Anemones, ranunculas, stocks and calendulas helped
to fill every corner with colour. The young rose bushes
were displaying their own special secrets of colour, form
and fragrance—each so different, each of unmatched beauty.

Simon was astonished: 'Had I not been here at the beginning,' he said, 'I'd never believe this garden is only six months old.'

I pointed out the more delicate species that he had averred would never grow in Jerusalem, especially not on Mount Zion. We paused before the three gerbera plants: the proud daisy-shaped flower heads, red, pink and yellow, stood high on their strong, straight slender stems.

I reminded Simon of his words when I brought them from Tel Aviv: 'They will never grow here, they need the humid heat and the sandy soil of the coastal plain.'

Simon was not at all scornful that day; he was unusually silent, and his friend seemed to be mumbling to himself.

We then went to look at the jacaranda tree. It had grown several feet higher, had sprouted many new leaves and was showing signs of the spreading branches soon to appear.

Simon lifted up his hands and said: 'I give in. You were right. Everything grows here.'

Later, when they thought I could not hear, I heard his friend say to Simon: 'How could she get things to grow like this?'

Simon replied with a shrug of his shoulders: 'She prays.'

They walked away in silence.

*   *   *

Some days later the borders were quiet again and life returned to normal. Early one morning, hearing singing voices and beating drums, I looked out of my window to see a procession which was coming through the small gate from the direction of David's Tomb and making its way to the shade of a very old mulberry tree near by. There, about forty men, women and children had gathered.

The scene became one of tremendous activity: some were busy spreading mats on which to sit, others were lighting small fires for cooking, while a seemingly endless number of food containers were being unpacked. Excited voices

E

were conversing, instructing, laughing. I went down to enquire what it was all about.

They were the members of one family from Iraq. Many were dressed in oriental clothes. I learned that the eldest son of the family had been seriously ill.

His wife told me: 'We took him to many doctors. They all said he could never get better and would not live long.'

His old parents were standing near her and listening closely.

'But we did not believe the doctors,' the old father said, his wrinkled face under his turban-style headgear smiling with satisfaction. 'We came here to ask King David to help us. The Almighty is greater than all the doctors.'

The mother nodded her agreement, lifting her hands and eyes heavenwards. 'Baruch haShem (Blessed be the Name), Baruch haShem,' she repeated several times.

'We came to Mount Zion every day to pray,' said the man's wife. 'We knew that King David would help us with our prayers and that the Almighty would cure my husband.'

Their faith had been acknowledged and the sick man had recovered completely. For this miracle of healing the whole family had now come together to Mount Zion to give thanks.

They prayed near David's Tomb all the morning and now, with the relative who had been restored to health in their midst, they were celebrating with great rejoicing. The young women were dancing some Eastern dances to the accompaniment of drum and song. The children were doing their share in adding to the noise.

The singing and the rhythmic beating of the drums continued until the close of day and as the muezzin finished calling the Moslems to prayer at sunset, silence again came to Mount Zion.

The Brotherhood of Goodwill

During the time that we had been living on Mount Zion, a small group of our friends in Jerusalem had grown together to form the nucleus of a Brotherhood of Goodwill. We came together one evening every month to exchange thoughts and aspirations.

We all shared the longing to see the fulfilment of the promise for peace on earth, and to participate, as far as was in our power, in the building up of this life of peace. Together we sought to learn from the Bible by study and contemplation, and to put what we had learnt into practice in our daily lives.

While friends from England and Germany were staying with us, sharing the same vision and drawn to us by the same spirit, we arranged an evening for all to meet together.

It was a very representative gathering. We ranged in age from under twenty to over eighty, and were drawn from many different circles of thought and belief. There were Jews, pious and orthodox, liberal and conservative; Christians, free and bound; a Jew who had become a Catholic priest and a Christian who had become a Jew—and there was also a Jew who, while believing in the Messiahship of Jesus, remained a devout Jew, united with his people, and was not connected with any church or Christian community.

Almost every path of the spiritual road was represented, but each one believed in the one God and was filled with His spirit—the spirit of love and goodwill, which united us all and made us one family—the children of God.

Among us were poets, musicians, teachers, business and professional men, housewives, priests and students. Five different languages were spoken, including Esperanto. Background, character, temperament and nationality were all so varied that it seemed impossible for such a mixed assembly to find any means of communication or unity.

The Esperantist, who was always advocating the importance of Esperanto, declared that evening: 'Well! Here you have an example of the need for a common language. How can you possibly get to know one another without it?'

Sitting next to him were two women, one a poet who

knew no German, the other a simple housewife from
Germany, who knew no other language. Smiling and happy,
their eyes shining, they had found some way of communi-
cating. They understood each other.

Girl students from England soon made contact with
Israeli students through music, song and dance. A poetess
read her poems in Hebrew. Someone who did not understand the language very well said to me: 'Although I did
not understand all the words, I seemed to understand the
spirit and that gave me much pleasure.'

The priest turned to the musician at his side, saying: 'How
is it possible that such a mixed group of people, some
meeting for the first time, can be so united, happy and
completely at ease?' The pious Jew on the other side of
him, hearing the remark, answered: 'The spirit of Zion has
descended upon us and made us one!' Then he turned to
the Esperantist: 'The language of the heart is far more
eloquent than the spoken word,' he said, and the Esperantist
had to admit that the language barrier had not marred the
joy or the unity of spirit at the gathering.

The over-eighty and the under-twenties joined hands in
dance and song. The pious Jew seemed to have an added
joy within him, he seemed to be looking into the future.

'What we see and feel here tonight,' he said, 'will one day
be experienced by all the world. The day when the Lord
promised: "I will pour out my spirit upon all flesh!".'

Shavuot

The seven weeks since the second day of Pesach had passed.
It was the eve of Shavuot, the Feast of Weeks, known to
the Christians as Pentecost.

Once again, pilgrims from all corners of the land were
climbing the steps to Mount Zion, to celebrate in the
vicinity of David's Tomb, as near as possible to the site
where the holy Temple had once stood.

They began arriving with their wives and children after midday. The bundles they carried on their shoulders included blankets and sleeping-bags, and in their hands were buckets and baskets packed with food and drinks. They had come to spend a night, or perhaps two, on Mount Zion.

The second night of Shavuot is traditionally recognized as the anniversary of David's death, and is spent reading the Psalms of David. For twenty-four hours the candle lit in his memory flickers above the heads of the worshippers.

Before the sun had set, I walked through the building in which the Tomb of David is housed. I had to be very careful where I stepped for in the dimly lit vaulted chambers, blanket-covered human forms were lying in all the corners and alcoves on the stone floors. Some slept from exhaustion after their long journey, others were making sure of their place for the night. Children ran about while mothers were unpacking their food and utensils. A long wooden table was being erected close to the Tomb. Here the men would sit all night, reading and praying.

Later, when the sun had gone and darkness hid us from the vigilance of the enemy, we again entered the dimly lit chambers of the old stone buildings. Within a few hours, the usual cold emptiness of these dark arched rooms had been transformed into the warmth and intimacy of a home.

Families sat around in circles on mats on the floor. Plates were being filled with food and there were cups for fruit drinks or wine. Some were singing folk-songs in the language of the country from which each had come. The children were singing the songs of Israel in Hebrew. An aged man, the lines on his face engraved by time and the sun, sat holding a small child on his knee. With welcoming eyes and a toothless smile, he beckoned me to sit beside him. His daughter, a woman well-on in years, offered me a plate of some spiced, exotic food.

'Come,' she said, 'share in our happiness.'

As I sat down beside the old man, his son told me in a mixture of French and Hebrew: 'We came from Morocco ten years ago. Every year on Shavuot we come here to thank the Almighty for bringing us to our Promised Land.'

In this family circle a girl who looked no more than sixteen was suckling a baby at her breast. The child was the old man's great-great grandson. The generations had come together for this pilgrimage from a distant village in the Negev.

'We like to spend Shavuot with King David,' one of the sons said. They all spoke of David as though he were physically present with them and had invited them to Mount Zion for this festival . . .

I walked among the other happy families squatting on the floor. Whatever their problems in Israel, they had been forgotten for this special occasion.

All through the night, the faint chanting of prayers could be heard, and mingled with the intermittent cries of children, the barking of dogs and the voices of people moving about in the darkness. I was conscious of the listening ears of the near-by Jordanian soldiers on guard duty and recognized the footsteps of our own soldiers.

The brightness of the stars waned as the first rosy flush of dawn suffused the eastern horizon, heralding sunrise and the approach of another day. The singing of the Chasidim on the roof of King David's Tomb marked the joyous end of the night of prayers. The sleepers were awakening and children were stirring with excitement in their unaccustomed surroundings. People from the city were arriving to join the worshippers. Soon the synagogues were filled and all around people were mingling and jostling together. Among them were also the tourists and sightseers, the onlookers who stood on the fringe of the joyous experience of those who were the 'guests' of King David.

Summer on Mount Zion

As Shavuot passed, Mount Zion settled down again to its customary peace. The echoes of the singing human voices continued for a while and then they too ceased. The birds sang as though in celebration of the fact that it was again a Sabbath morning. It was summer on Mount Zion.

Through the open window came the scented breath of the garden. I looked out at the hills and valleys basking in the sun's warmth.

In Garden Square, just outside our gate, a man stood silently contemplating the vista before him. His thick mop of brown curly hair and his full beard seemed to enlarge the size of the head upon his broad shoulders; although short in stature, his strong muscular figure gave the impression of power, strength and vitality. David Palombo stood relaxed on this Sabbath morning beside his sculpture 'Wings', just near our gate. As with all his works, he had succeeded in imprinting his personality on it. The impressive power with which the flames and ashes of satanic torture and murder were symbolically expressed in the door of Yad Vashem, the memorial to the Holocaust, was in complete contrast to the sensitive delicacy of some of his smaller works on exhibition in the Gallery. In these, cold hard iron had been transformed into forms and patterns of such beauty that they stirred within one the same joy as a tracery of leaves against the sky, a butterfly clinging to the heart of a flower, or a sensuous curve carved by nature.

I went down to the garden. David looked over the railings. 'You've a beautiful garden,' he said. 'I could never make a garden like this, but then you could not produce my sculpture, so we'll each keep to that for which we have talent and enjoy each other's works.' His smile lit up his whole face and as always brought a twinkle to his eyes.

Yona came out of the Gallery carrying little Paulita, and David went to fetch her pram. This was their day of rest and with Paulita comfortably seated in her baby carriage, gazing blissfully at the big world around her, the proud and happy parents strolled down the road pushing the pram.

I watched them walk slowly down the road normally used for military traffic. Across the border the Jordanian soldiers were also watching. The peace of the Sabbath had cast its spell over the scene as though some unseen power would take the men's hands off their loaded guns and put them in their neighbours' hands instead, in a clasp of friendship and goodwill.

As the sun warmed the Sabbath morning, I saw the figure of Rabbi Twilensky coming from the direction of David's Tomb. On his head was a fur-brimmed hat. His long, blue-silk Sabbath caftan glistened in the sunshine. With his quick, light step he reached our door and came in with his usual happy smile.

'Shabbat Shalom,' he called as he entered the gate. His long side locks were carefully curled and his clean white shirt could be seen through his beard. I wondered anew how anyone could emerge from the one small damp room in which he lived with his family in that state of trimness and happiness.

For Rabbi Twilensky the Sabbath was a day of reverence and respect, a day of joy and gladness. He saw the world as his Creator had done on the seventh day—'*He saw that it was good*'. We stood on the balcony, looking across the hills and valleys to the distant mountains shrouded in the morning haze, and we both saw that '*it was good*'.

'If only the heart of mankind could be filled with that goodness!' I said with a deep sigh.

'When the Messiah comes,' said Rabbi Twilensky, 'then we shall have peace on earth.'

'How do you think of the Messiah?' I asked him. He was very quiet for some moments. Then, looking down at the garden beneath us, he said: 'You've a very beautiful garden here on Mount Zion, full of flowers. It is like the family

of King David. Every member of his family is good, just
as every flower in your garden is beautiful. But there is
one flower in David's garden which is more beautiful than
any other, even too beautiful for this earth, so it is kept
in heaven until mankind is ready to receive it.'

After a little pause, he said: 'God asks us to keep his
commandments, to be obedient to the Torah and then He
will send that "flower" from heaven, the Messiah who will
bring peace on earth.'

As we talked two guests arrived, a lady from Jerusalem
with a friend from England on her first visit to Israel.
Fearing the walk on the road, under the surveillance of the
Jordanian and our own soldiers, they had climbed the steps
and now stood on our balcony facing the enemy military
post.

The much-surprised English visitor remarked: 'How can
you live so near the border and not be afraid?'

'So many Israelites live close to borders,' I replied. 'There
is no place for fear in Israel. Work has to be done, develop-
ing, building, making the land fruitful and defending the
homeland. Faith dispels fear.'

Soon we were joined by Albert and a few members of
the congregation of the little synagogue after the Sabbath
service. It was becoming customary to say Kiddush at Ha-
Ohel after the morning service.

For Rabbi Twilensky just singing was not enough; his
body demanded an outward expression of his inner joy. He
began to dance to the rhythm of his song.

Before long he was joined by the white-bearded Ya'acov,
his pockets bulging with Bibles, the red-bearded Chasid,
the black-bearded Rabbi from Poland, Albert and others
who, holding hands, danced together in a circle, their voices
filling the room with song.

'I had read about such things in writings on Chasidic
life,' the English woman commented, 'but I would never
have believed that they still happen or that I would ever

witness and share in such an expression of Sabbath joy. I'm really touched—it seems to bring to life some deep-seated Jewish consciousness, which I hadn't even known I possessed.'

As this singing and dancing were going on, I looked through the window to see another large group waiting at our gate. I ran down to the door to discover that these new visitors were a group of German Christians.

They had come to Israel to build a rest home at Shavei Zion, on the north coast near Nahariya, a small town built by the Jews fleeing Hitler. Here, as in their first rest-home in Nahariya itself, anyone who had suffered at the hands of the Nazis was a welcome guest. No payment was accepted. With selfless devotion and often at great personal sacrifice, these Germans were atoning for what had happened to the German Jews.

They had come to spend the Sabbath in Jerusalem, and one of the group who had already paid us a visit had brought them to greet us. It flashed through my mind that there would not be room enough upstairs for all of them, and also that this intrusion might disturb the spontaneity of the dancing and singing upstairs. I took the German group into a room downstairs, one immediately below that in which the orthodox group were, and served them drinks and refreshments.

Soon they, too, began to express their happiness in song —hymns and psalms in German. They prayed for the peace of Jerusalem.

'This is the first time,' one of the women said, 'that we have felt so free and happy in a Jewish home, that we are not being made conscious of our German nationality and our Christian faith.'

At the end of the Sabbath, with Jerusalem glowing golden in the late afternoon sun, another group of some thirty-five people was making its way slowly to our front door. Americans this time. Gilbert, Rabbi of a Reform Temple in the United States, was conducting some members of his congregation on a tour of Israel. He had spent some days with us on a previous visit, and loved Israel and Mount Zion.

He, his wife and his children were all deeply imbued with American values, their way of life orientated to American standards. Gilbert had found his place in America as the spiritual leader of a reform synagogue. He ministered to the needs of a congregation, the members of which loved him. His was a satisfying and a full life, he had always thought —a life comparatively free of problems. That was until Jerusalem had spun its golden thread about him, from which he was in fact never to disentangle himself.

Gilbert had always been drawn to Jerusalem. On a previous visit he had told me: 'I come to Jerusalem at every opportunity—for a month, a week, or even only a day.'

'What draws you here so strongly?' I had asked him.

'My spiritual hunger,' he had replied. 'I come here starved for the spiritual food I can get only in Jerusalem, and I return with my soul and my spirit replenished.'

'Don't you want to live here?' I had asked him.

'Of course,' he had replied, 'but I have to think of my family—it would be hard for me to find work here. The reform synagogue is not at all popular in Israel.' Embarrassed, he continued: 'My children aren't happy when they come here. There is the language difficulty, the different values of life and the lower standard of living.'

'That would not represent any real barrier,' I had said, 'children soon adjust themselves.'

Shaking his head dubiously, he had answered: 'But I have a responsibility to my congregation,' adding somewhat defensively, 'and I like my work there.'

Gilbert's inner conflict had still to be resolved. And now he stood again at our door, saying with a smile: 'Another opportunity to come to Jerusalem and Mount Zion! So I had to bring these good people to meet you and visit Ha-Ohel. May we come in?'

The thirty-five people crowded into our upstairs lounge. They sat on chairs, on tables, in the window embrasures and on the floor. The view through the open door leading on to the balcony fascinated all of them. Many commented on the landscape, its beauty, the sense of peace in the room. Others were silent, finding no words to express their emotions.

As the sun began to set, it first intensified the colours of the mountains and illuminated the sky. Between the golden hills of Judea and the pastel-coloured mountains of Moab, part of the large expanse of the Dead Sea could be seen as a tiny blue jewel in the distance. Then the heads of the Jordanian soldiers above their sand-bagged fortifications appeared as two small black balls against this background of pastel and gold, reminders of man's intrusion in God's perfect creation.

The light gradually faded, the shadows deepened and the stars began to shimmer brightly as the voices in the room joined in song. Gilbert and I read some psalms, with their many references to Mount Zion. Gilbert then performed the Havdala service. The new week had begun!

Chapter Four

The Seventh Month

The sun-browned hills and the ripening seed pods in the garden foretold the approaching end of summer, preparing to hand over the ministration of the earth's needs to autumn. We were coming to the first day of the seventh month in the Jewish calendar, the month of Tishri which corresponds to the months of September-October in the Gregorian calendar.

It was the time of preparation for the three important festivals which are celebrated at this season—Rosh Hashanah (New Year), Yom Kippur (Day of Atonement) and Succoth (Feast of Tabernacles).

In the Bible we read: *'And the Lord spoke unto Moses, saying, speak unto the Children of Israel saying: In the seventh month, in the first day of the month, shall ye have a sabbath, a memorial of blowing of trumpets, an holy convocation.*

'Also on the tenth day of this seventh month, there shall be a day of Atonement: it shall be an holy convocation to you, and ye shall afflict your souls. . . .

'On the fifteenth day of this seventh month shall be the Feast of Tabernacles for seven days unto the Lord.'

Rosh Hashanah

The days preceding Rosh Hashanah are a time for soul searching, days when Jews assemble in their synagogues to recite slichot (penitential prayers). On Mount Zion the voices of the little assembly in the synagogue could be heard daily singing these prayers. The words of the Psalm:

'God is near to all who call upon Him' opened the heavens to all their supplications.

At this time, an unexpected stranger arrived at our door. An Englishman sent to us by a mutual friend who had visited Ha-Ohel earlier in the year. As Gregory introduced himself, I realized that he was the son of a distinguished English family.

'What has brought you to Israel at this time?' I asked him.

'To learn something from Judaism,' he replied, and then went on to explain: 'You see, I belong to the Anglican Church. My family have been members of this Church for many generations. But in recent years I've felt a growing dissatisfaction with it and, in particular, its attitude towards the Jews.'

He paused for a while and then continued: 'I have begun to believe that if I want to understand more about my own faith I must come and learn from the Jews. I feel that only in the treasure store of Judaism will I find the understanding that I am seeking of my own Christian faith.'

'That is quite an unusual statement from a Christian,' I said.

His clear blue eyes grew more serious. 'I've felt an inner compulsion to come to Israel and to live for a time with the Jewish people.' He looked at me questioningly, 'May I join you in the celebration of the festivals of this coming month?'

'Of course, you are very welcome.'

Somewhere on Mount Zion the shofar could be heard practising for the coming festivals. Across the iron fence, Arab soldiers were firing their guns at unknown targets in the distance. It was the eve of Rosh Hashanah.

Gregory was with us. 'This is a great experience for me,' he said.

'I suppose you know, Gregory, that these festival days which you have come to share with us are the most important and the most solemn of all Jewish Holy Days.'

'Tell me something about them,' he said. 'Doesn't the Bible tell us that New Year is *"a day of blowing the trumpets"*?'

'Yes, the blowing of the shofar is the central point in the observance of this festival. It is the clarion call to the slumbering conscience. We are required to take stock of our deeds, our thoughts, every step, every action, every transgression, so that we may review our conduct for the past year and repent, resolving to do better in the coming year. New Year's day is a day of reckoning, when it is believed that the "Book of Life and Death" is open before the Lord.'

'Most other festivals have some historic significance,' said Gregory. 'This seems different.'

'You are right,' I replied. 'This day of reckoning is concerned mainly with man's relationship with God and his fellow-men, yet the prayers in its liturgy are not just for the Jew, they are most closely related to creation as a whole.'

Gregory joined Albert and the small congregation which had assembled in the little synagogue on Mount Zion. The numbers were small because of the restrictions on visiting Mount Zion by night, but there were always the very devout few who risked all dangers to be here on this solemn occasion. They chanted the prayers of the evening service and it seemed as if the very depths of their hearts were unlocked as they communed with their Maker.

After the service, walking back to Ha-Ohel, Gregory, silent and thoughtful, had a far-away look on his face.

'Never have I experienced the nearness of God as I felt it this evening in that little synagogue,' he said.

He was to spend the night with us, as he wished to be on Mount Zion for the whole of the first day of Rosh Hashanah, in his search for understanding.

'How different the celebrations of our New Year have been in London,' he mused. 'Sometimes we went to a short church service at midnight, but parties were the main thing. We drank and danced as we welcomed in the New Year at midnight. It is also strange to find that your New Year begins at sunset and in the seventh month.'

'It may seem strange,' I answered, 'but I always understand it this way. The Bible tells us that ". . . *the evening and the morning were the first day*". From this we understand that the evening is the beginning of the day; likewise the autumn or the seventh month is the beginning of the year Before we come to the light of day we have to pass through the darkness of night. And before new life surges in the spring, it is prepared deep in the earth, through the rains and storms of winter.'

Gregory nodded thoughtfully, and I continued: 'So it is also with man, who after passing through the dark night of suffering and trial, emerges into the light, the dawn of understanding, compassion and love.'

'I've never thought of it that way,' said Gregory, and remained very thoughtful.

It was almost midnight when we all retired for the first night of the year, wishing one another 'shanah tova'—a happy new year.

The next morning, during the service, we listened to the blowing of the shofar in the synagogue. Although on this day it was sounded as a call to introspection and repentance, the readings in the liturgy also told us of its joyous significance on other occasions: in praise of the King; when the returned exiles again worship the Lord on the Holy Mountain in Jerusalem; and when the greatest trumpet of all is sounded to announce the coming of the Messiah.

Yom Kippur

Mount Zion was enveloped in a mystic aura on the day of preparation for Yom Kippur, the Day of Atonement, the hallowed day which draws all Jews to the synagogue, even those who observe little of Jewish tradition or the Jewish festivals at other times. It is as if a shofar blown in the heavens stirs the conscience of every Jew, making him aware of his need for repentance, atonement and forgiveness.

There was a hushed stillness as I went up on the roof of King David's Tomb. There I heard an old Rabbi pouring out his anguished petitions, always facing in the direction of the Temple Mount. He told me how he had prayed at the sacred wall of the Temple for many years until 1948, when the Arabs gained control of the Old City of Jerusalem. His deep longing to be there again, the impassioned appeal for the restoration and rebuilding of the Temple rang out in the stillness.

On my way down from the roof, the question arose again in my mind: How long? How long before Jerusalem would be liberated and we could walk freely to the holy places? I remembered the reply Ya'acov had once given me: 'As long as the Creator wills . . .'.

As I was preparing the last meal before sundown, after which the twenty-four hour fast would begin, I saw Gregory walking slowly up the hill, then standing before our gate in deep contemplation. He seemed to be held by the magic of the atmosphere on Mount Zion on the eve of this hallowed day.

He was very quiet at the meal as though sensing that he was about to experience something of the depths of the Jewish faith. As I cleared away the remains of the meal, I said to him: 'You may eat whatever you like tomorrow, it is not necessary for you to fast.' He looked very surprised and answered: 'Of course I intend to fast. How can I share this festival if I do not enter into it wholly?'

The sun was sinking behind the Mount of Olives, and Mount Zion was aglow with gold, waiting in silence for the small band of worshippers who would be coming for the 'Kol Nidre' evening service with which Yom Kippur begins. 'Kol Nidre' literally means 'all the vows', and is a plea to be absolved from all unfulfilled vows made to the Lord.

F

The little synagogue was filled to capacity. There were many new faces. The solemnity and significance of the occasion seemed to permeate the very stones of the old walls.

The Cantor, enveloped in his prayer shawl which left only his face uncovered, began to chant the prayers. As his impassioned voice rang out with the stirring, haunting melody of the Kol Nidre prayer, it seemed as if we were fused with all our Jewish brethren the world over. This sense of communion remained with us as we left the synagogue.

The Cantor was an elderly man with a blond-white beard and kind blue eyes. He returned with us to Ha-Ohel, silently wrapped in his own thoughts. A bed was prepared for him for the night. At daybreak he would again be in the synagogue where he remained for the whole day, chanting the prayers until after sundown when the fast ended.

The next morning, Gregory accompanied Albert to the synagogue where the congregation was assembling for prayer. Only those for whom Mount Zion had a very special meaning would have undertaken the long walk from their homes to climb up to this Holy Mount on a fast day. Many, including Albert, never moved out of the synagogue the whole day, but when I went out for a short break I met Gregory: 'Taking a breath of fresh air,' as he put it. The warm air of the crowded synagogue and his first experience of fasting had been a little difficult for him.

'It's quite amazing,' he said, 'to see these devout Jews praying, oblivious to any physical needs, and unaware of any movement or sound about them.'

'Yes,' I replied, 'this is a very solemn day for all Jews.'

Together we climbed the steps to the roof of King David's Tomb, and looked towards the area where the Temple had once stood.

The part of the morning service we had just read was still fresh in our minds. It had dealt with the ordinances for this day at the time the Temple was still standing.

'Just imagine it all,' said Gregory. 'The High Priest garbed in his holy white linen coat, tied with a linen girdle and wearing his linen mitre. How did it go?'

' "*He shall take two goats and present them before the Lord at the door of the Tabernacle*",' I filled in for him.

'Oh! Yes,' he continued, 'that was the "sin offering" in atonement for himself, his family and the whole Jewish people.'

We were silent for a while. 'And we're looking across to the very site where it all occurred,' I added.

* * *

'Look!' Gregory exclaimed, as he drew me with him into his imaginary journey into the past. 'Imagine we're at the Temple on the Day of Atonement. Now we're entering the Temple court among a great press of people; our attention is riveted on the High Priest in white linen raiment, preparing to enter the Tabernacle — "The Holy of Holies".'

'Yes,' I replied, 'and I can even see the bulls and goats passing through the gates.' Gregory's vivid imagination was helping to set the scene for me.

'We're sharing in the tremendous sense of awe,' he said quickly. 'The High Priest enters the innermost sanctuary of the Temple, alone, to sprinkle blood upon the altar and make atonement for all our sins.'

* * *

I think we both returned from that fanciful flight into the past with a feeling of relief that atonement now involves the offering of a repentant heart, rather than the blood of animals.

Gregory was silent for quite a long time before he spoke again: 'The Jews no longer have a High Priest to intercede for them with a blood sacrifice in atonement for their sins. But Christians believe that their "High Priest" is now in the sanctuary of heaven and having made atonement for their sins with his own blood, intercedes for them directly before the Throne of God.'

'Yes,' I replied, 'that marked the separation of Christianity from its parent, Judiasm. Jews can't accept the one whom Christians regard as their High Priest; nor do they accept that by his blood atonement was made for the collective sin of the world.'

Gregory continued as we descended the steps on our way back to the synagogue: 'You know, the mystery of the blood sacrifice has lately been occupying my mind a great deal. The Bible tells us that when Moses gave the God-given laws and instructions to the Children of Israel, he said: "*The life of the flesh is in the blood and I have given it to you upon the altar to make atonement for your souls, for it is the blood that maketh atonement for the soul!*" How do the Jews regard this now?'

'There are many different schools of thought in Judaism,' I replied. 'The teaching that "atonement is through blood" can be found in the Talmud, and strictly orthodox Jewry believes that with the restoration of the Temple there will again be animal sacrifices for the cleansing of our sins.'

'But others feel differently?' Gregory asked.

'Yes,' I continued. 'I suppose the most widely held belief is that sacrifices came to an end with the destruction of the Temple; inevitable, since they could not be offered elsewhere. There has been a spiritual development of Judaism which would seem to preclude the re-introduction of animal sacrifice.'

'I'm not sure that I understand you.'

'Let's take as an example the liturgy of today's festival,' I replied. 'The emphasis there is on the spiritual values of atonement through repentance, return to God and fasting as an expression of curbing the physical appetites and the gratification of the senses. Humility, devotion and charity are required. We need to love our fellow-men as we are all equal before God.'

'Yes, I see what you mean and I agree with all that, but of course the mystery, the use of blood in atonement still remains.'

'We are now touching the pulse and trying to probe the depths of a mystery which is beyond our understanding,' I concluded, 'and can only be approached, accepted or rejected according to the measure of our faith.'

We returned to the synagogue, where we remained until, with the shadows lengthening at the end of the day, the deeply impressive concluding service of Yom Kippur was chanted by the Rabbi and the standing congregation.

After a day calling for contrition and humility, with physical dependence on spiritual food alone, the fervent last appeal for forgiveness and the affirmation of God's mercy and sovereignty seemed to me to be wrung from *the very depths of the soul: 'Oh blot out and remove our transgressions and sins from thy sight . . . And may our eyes behold thy return to Zion. Blessed art thou, O Lord, who restorest thy divine presence unto Zion.'*

Then the clear single call of the shofar announced the end of the fast and the return to everyday life.

We invited a number of the congregants to Ha-Ohel to break their fast with us before they began their return to their more distant homes. The solemnity of the day still held us all in its spell as we took our first drink and food for twenty-four hours.

When Gregory left us that night, he seemed like a man who had journeyed not only to attend the Temple festival in Biblical times, or the simple service held that day, but had been down the shaft of his own soul and discovered new mysteries in its depth. All he managed to say when he left was:

'D'you know, I think I really felt the embrace of Zion for the stranger in its midst.'

Succoth

The solemn festivals were over and now came the week of preparation for the third, the festival of rejoicing: Succoth—the Feast of Tabernacles or Booths, also known as the Feast of the Ingathering of the Harvest.

'*On the fifteenth day of the seventh month, when ye have gathered in the yield of your land ye shall observe the festival of the Lord seven days. . . . On the first day ye shall take the produce of goodly trees, branches of palm trees, boughs of thick trees and willows of the brook and ye shall rejoice before the Lord your God seven days . . . ye shall live in booths seven days . . . that future genera- tions may know that I made the Children of Israel to live in booths when I brought them out of the Land of Egypt . . . I am the Lord your God.*'

Gregory was with us again, and I explained to him that it was customary to begin to build these booths on balconies, roofs or in courtyards immediately after Yom Kippur had ended. Early in the morning after Yom Kippur, Obadiah who fed the pigeons on Mount Zion, brought the wooden poles for the little booth (succah) which was to be built on our front balcony.

And life was returning to normal again. It was good to see the Palombo jeep bringing David, Yona and Paulita back to Mount Zion. They had spent the festivals with their relatives. A small group of tourists stood close to our gate in Garden Square, looking in silent wonder towards the Judean Hills. The sun shone on the fluttering wings of the pigeons circling the red-tiled roof of the little museum. Two white doves alighted on the iron railings of the garden wall over which the bougainvillaea was spilling clusters of crimson flowers.

The peace and quiet on Mount Zion seemed to have a special quality these days, as though all the prayers of the previous days had, ascending from here, opened the windows of heaven through which blessings now descended.

As the light turned to gold one of these late afternoons, David came into the square with his little daughter on his shoulders. 'I'll show you something you've never seen before,' he boasted, as he very gently put Paulita down on to her feet. Grasping her father's hand, and swaying unsteadily, running rather than walking, she was chuckling with delight. David's face beamed with pride as he withdrew his hand from her clasp, and he watched his daughter take a few independent steps and then land with a bump on the ground.

'She still needs your hand,' I said to David.

'Soon she will be managing without it,' he replied. 'After all, a few falls are a small price to pay for independence.'

Yona came out to rescue Paulita and David mounted his scooter, racing noisily down the road. 'That is the only noise we have to remind us of the outside world,' I said to Yona as we watched him disappear down the hill. 'What a blessing it is that no motor traffic is allowed to come up here to disturb the peace.'

'It may not be for long,' Yona replied. 'There are rumours that the road to Mount Zion is to be widened and opened to all public vehicles.'

The preparations for Succoth went forward apace. There was much activity in the courtyard of the Sephardic synagogue adjoining King David's Tomb. A large booth was being erected for the pilgrims who would come to Mount Zion during the seven days of the Feast of Tabernacles. Smaller booths were also being set up in the open space under the bent pine trees and 'palm branches and boughs of goodly trees' were already being cut for roofs.

As Obadiah was completing the booth on our balcony, we heard shots being fired near by. It was not an unusual occurrence, but as always it left us feeling rather troubled. Where had they been shooting, and at whom? It was only later in the evening, when Efraim and Danny, two of the Nahal soldiers came to visit us, that we learnt what had happened. The Arabs about a quarter of a mile away along the border, had without provocation, fired on a block of flats in the vicinity of the Notre Dame Convent. A young Jewish girl sitting on the balcony of her home had been seriously wounded; a Christian working in the convent workshop had been killed. For the citizens of Jerusalem these incidents were like dark threads woven into the pattern of their daily lives.

The wooden frame for the booth on the balcony had been completed. The palm leaves and other branches had been laid across the upper supports to make the green leafy roof through which the sky, the heavenly roof, could be seen. Harvest fruits were hung from the beams to decorate the little booth: grapes, pomegranates, apples, lemons and dates. I had cut out an opening in the burlap material nailed to the supports to make a little window looking on to the Kidron Valley and the Judean Hills. The Jordanian military post facing us seemed nearer than ever, and the heads of the Arab soldiers above their sand-bagged roof were always visible.

Danny, who had come to help me finish the decorations and arrange the table and the seating, said: 'You shouldn't have made the window there. When you have the light on at night it will attract attention and the Arabs will be able to see everything you do.'

'We might as well continue to provide them with a little interest,' I replied, for I had been conscious of their curiosity over our activities while constructing the booth.

Ya'acov arrived with a contribution to the decorations— a picture of the Tabernacle in the wilderness surrounded by the tents of the twelve tribes of Israel, and he proceeded to pin this painstakingly on to the flimsy wall.

Rabbi Twilensky also came to look into the little booth and said a prayer of thanksgiving and blessing. 'During these seven days of Succoth you will surely have a heavenly visitor here each day to bless you,' was his comment of appreciation as he left. As always he seemed to be dancing, rather than walking, down the stairs.

A few clouds hovering above the horizon were caught by the last rays of the sun as the Festival of Tabernacles began, and we sang: '*You, Lord, our God, have graciously given us holidays for gladness, and festive seasons for joy: this Feast of Tabernacles, our festival of rejoicing, a holy convocation in remembrance of the exodus from Egypt.*'

The members of our Nahal family who were not on duty joined us, as did Ya'acov and Gregory. The lights were kindled in the booth. Albert said the blessing on the wine, and after songs and prayers we partook of our first meal in the flower-and-fruit-filled booth. The soldiers were uneasy, knowing the Arabs were watching.

Looking up we saw the stars shining through the leaves and Ya'acov said: 'It is good that the Creator reminds us that the only permanent roof over our heads is the heavenly one.'

As the singing continued, I wondered what the Jordanian soldiers were thinking. I wished I could have invited them to join us.

Ya'acov expressed a longing to sleep in the booth that night.

'But there is only this hard narrow bench,' I exclaimed. 'It is hardly possible to sleep here and there is no room for anything more comfortable.' But Ya'acov slept that night in the booth, lying on his back on the hard narrow bench, his Bibles on the table beside him.

After morning prayers the following day I served breakfast in the booth. Ya'acov claimed he had slept superbly: 'What greater joy and blessing could I ask for than to have a night in a booth on this Holy Mount, this place where in the future people from all nations will come to celebrate the Feast of Tabernacles?' He smiled at Gregory. 'Today we have the first one from the nations who has come to celebrate with us. Blessed be the Creator who fulfils all His promises.'

There was also an amusing incident this first Succoth we spent on Mount Zion. One day the sound of a car coming up the road drew us to the window. We saw the familiar white United Nations car with U.N. in large black letters on its side. It stopped at our front gate and two men got out and came to the door. Albert and I looked at each other questioningly.

The two 'United Nations' representatives apologized for intruding as they entered our upstairs lounge. They glanced towards the closed door leading to the balcony as we invited them to be seated, and one of them rather embarrassedly explained the reason for their visit.

'We've had complaints from the Jordanians that new military fortifications were being built here on Mount Zion, and we were sent to investigate.'

Albert and I suppressed our smiles with difficulty. 'You're welcome to investigate all our activities here,' I said. 'It's true that we've been doing some construction on our balcony facing the Jordanian positions.'

The two men stood close behind me as I opened the door to reveal the gaily decorated booth with its open garlanded window overlooking the Jordanian military post.

'This is our new fortification,' we said, and they joined us in our laughter as they looked through the window at the heads of the Arab soldiers behind the sandbags not many yards away.

They drank a glass of wine with us in the booth, listening with interest to our explanation of the symbolism of the decorations. Before they left, they asked if they could visit us again, bringing some of their colleagues with them.

The seven days of the Feast of Tabernacles, were all days of pilgrimage to Mount Zion. Each day they came— from all corners of Israel and from distant lands. Singing and dancing they celebrated the feast of rejoicing, taking their food and drink in the little booths provided for them.

Many friends and strangers came to Ha-Ohel to drink a glass of wine in our little booth. Many of them appeared ill at ease, aware of the ever-present danger visible through the open window. But nothing could mar Ya'acov's joy.

'For me,' he said, 'it merely adds meaning to the festival. It is a reminder of our deliverance from Egypt, and the protection of the Almighty in the face of danger.'

The hills were now brown and parched. The earth had offered up the fullness of its fruit, and the garden had spent its strength in the amorous embrace of summer. All nature seemed to stretch invisible hands upwards in supplication for water.

On the seventh day of the feast of Tabernacles, special prayers for rain are offered up. Up the precarious old steps to the roof of the synagogue climbed the congregation—a small band of men, prayer shawls over their shoulders, open prayer books in their hands, and ritual skull-caps on their heads. They stood facing the Temple area in the Old City, quite oblivious of the dangers to which they had exposed themselves. For besides the Jordanian soldiers at the military post we knew there were others hidden behind the nearby trees.

'I will prepare my inward thoughts, to pray for water,' the men chanted on the roof. 'I will deliberate a little before I proceed to speak of the moistening work of the creation of water. . . .'

A shot rang out. The men did not pause in their chanting: 'Thou hast retained in thy hand the key of the water; so that no one hath power, without thy leave, to open the treasure of water; send altogether a favourable, and liberal purifying rain.'

The men bowed their heads in silence for a while, and then continued: '. . . He hath ordained that the clouds should bear the burden of the waters; they move and fly in the open firmament of heaven; they remain collected till they are permitted to pour out the water. . . .'

The chanting continued: 'The parched earth is softened by the descent of the dropping water; the thirsty fields which the scorching summer heat hath parched are satiated with water. . . . For thou art the Lord our God. Who causeth the wind to blow and the rain to descend—for blessing and not for a curse; for life and not for death; for plenty and not for famine.'

I looked at the blue heavens where little clouds moved 'in the open firmament', and gathered overhead. As the service was ending, I felt a little drop of water on my face. I saw the tiny wet spots on the roof.

The rains had come—even as the men were still praying. I remembered the words of Isaiah: '*And it shall come to pass that before they call I will answer and while they are yet speaking I will hear.*'

That night Gregory came to have the last meal in our little booth with us. The seven days of 'dwelling in booths' had ended.

'Is this the end of the Festival?' he asked.

'No,' I replied. 'It is written that "the eighth day shall be an holy convocation unto you; it is a solemn assembly, ye shall do no servile work therein". This night is Simchath Torah—the Rejoicing of the Law. In most synagogues and in the streets, people are now gathering around the rabbis. They are carrying the Torah Scrolls. Tonight they'll dance and sing with ecstatic joy.'

The Rejoicing of the Law marked the end of the festive cycle of the seventh month, and Gregory, summing up his experiences during his stay with us, pointed out: 'You know of course that the Feast of Tabernacles differs from the others in one important respect. It is to become an international festival, the one involving all the nations and not just the chosen people.'

'Yes,' I replied. 'The Bible foretells that all the families of the earth "*shall even go up from year to year to worship the King, the Lord of Hosts, and to keep the Feast of Tabernacles*".'

Chapter Five

The days were growing shorter. The garden was preparing for its winter sleep as the soaking winter rains set in. The cycle of the year's festivals from our first Hanukka on Mount Zion had, moving with the seasons, run its course, and once again we were approaching Hanukka—the beginning of another cycle.

We remembered the first Hanukka which we had shared with Ya'acov and the Nahal boys: the endless supply of potato fritters, and Tamar's birthday cake; the fierce storm that had raged outside and the strong sense of peace and security that enclosed us as we sat in the house. . . .

We were together again and new friends had joined the familiar faces around the table to celebrate the festival.

A Hanukka Story

On the first day of Hanukka, I stood at our window and watched two figures coming up the hill. They were walking slowly, a tall young man supporting a small, frail, elderly woman, the sleeves of whose buttoned coat hung empty at her sides. I watched, drawn to them in some indefinable way, as they approached the Chamber of Martyrs and then went down the steps to its entrance.

Some time later as I came up from the garden, I saw the same couple approaching our gate. The woman looked even more frail than before, if that was possible, and her wrinkled cheeks were still wet with tears.

The young man stopped. 'Could I trouble you for a glass of water for my friend?' he asked.

'Of course,' I replied, and I invited them inside.

He accepted gratefully and gently led his companion into our house. When they were seated in the lounge, I brought them water. He took the glass and put it to the lips of his companion, delicately and with infinite care, so that she might drink.

'Wouldn't you both like to rest for a while?'

'I think it would be a good idea,' he said, looking at his companion. 'Thank you! My name,' he continued, 'is Haim Yasur. My friend is Frau Braun. Her English is not very good, but she understands.'

At the mention of her name, the woman's face was transformed by a smile of greeting. The room was warm. She stood up, and as he removed her coat, the sleeves of her simple dress hung empty at her sides. I left them sitting together while I made some tea and sandwiches, which I thought they might like.

Again I was deeply impressed with the love that he showed her as he helped her to sip her tea, and eat a little of the sandwich.

Impelled by more than ordinary curiosity, I said: 'May I ask what brought you here? Mount Zion is a very special place for me.'

I saw them exchange glances, the woman's slight nod.

'Well,' said the tall young man, 'we came today to kindle a light before the ashes in the Chamber of the Martyrs in memory of our dear departed ones. It is a long story if you have the patience to listen to it.'

'Please do tell me,' I replied.

Haim began: 'I came to this country at the age of seventeen, together with a number of other lads rescued from the concentration camps in Germany.'

I had seen some of these concentration camp survivors in London, before I came to Israel, their bodies weakened, their minds clouded, or forever warped by their experiences in labour camps or death camps.

'What happened when you arrived in Israel?' I asked.

'We were taken to a kibbutz, where with loving care so many of us were made near-whole again. Now I am happily married with two children.' But he hastily added, 'Of course, that is another story. . . .'

I shall now recount the story I pieced together from Haim Yasur's account that morning:

Every eve of Hanukka he had the same dream in which his mother appeared to him. And he would wake each time with her words ringing in his ears, 'Go and look for Angel! . . . Look for Angel!' When he first had the dream he had not taken much notice of it. Angel was surely dead, and in any case he could not possibly go and look for her at that time.

Hanukka was always a soul-stirring time for him. Memories buried deep within him were revived by his mother's voice. In latter years the dream had begun to torment him and gave him no peace. By then he had saved enough money for the journey, and after celebrating Hanukka with his family he set out to obey his mother's command.

For many months he searched all likely places in Germany —offices holding records of Nazi victims, hospitals, institutions. He found no trace of Angel. His money had run out and his family in Israel was deeply troubled by his long absence. Was it a disturbance of the mind driving him on this seemingly hopeless quest? Was he a fool chasing a phantom? Haim asked himself these and many other questions, but found himself unable to give up and go home. He took whatever work he could find and continued to search. He could not rest.

Soon it would be Hanukka again. Once more he was drawn to his small home town where had last seen Angel. It had been destroyed and rebuilt, and he had already searched there in vain.

He stood gazing at a new building. How long he had been there, he did not know. In his mind's eye he saw only the old house which had once stood on this site, the house from which the Nazis had taken them away—him, his mother, his lovely sister Sara and his two little brothers. . . .

A poor widow had lived there. It was she who had seen his father dragged off by the Nazis from their home a few doors away, while the family had been out shopping. And it was she who had run to warn them not to return home but to come to her after nightfall. She had kept them hidden in her cellar for many months, fed them and ministered to their needs. They had called her Angel: the Germans later called her traitor—Judenfreund.

It was the eve of Hanukka, and Angel had a surprise for them. She had found an old menorah—an eight-branched Hanukka candlestick. She took some candles from her Christmas tree, and she had baked a cake with ingredients she had in some miraculous way collected. After securely shutting all doors and windows, she took these treasures down to the cellar. She then made sure that every crack through which a light might be seen was sealed, and she closed the barred door with extra care. But Angel had not noticed as she descended the stairs that a suspicious neighbour had been crouching unseen in a dark corner at the entrance.

They sat around the makeshift table in the cellar—the mother, Sara, the two little boys, Angel and Haim. Haim kindled the first Hanukka light with the prayer his father had taught him as a small boy, and they told stories about the light and the miracle of the light and the Lord's deliverance. They spoke about the courage of the Maccabees, who had been ready to fight and to die for their faith in the God of Israel rather than surrender to the worshippers of idols. The family forgot their own plight for a while and were inspired with new hope and courage. They saw the tears in Angel's eyes, shining like stars in heaven and felt the love which flowed from heart to heart.

But outside the floodgates of Hell had been opened and the rivers gushing blood knew no bounds. Then they heard heavy footsteps on the stairs. The barricaded door was pounded open; the swastikas on several arm bands were revealed in the last flickering of the Hanukka light.

Cruel hands grabbed the mother clutching her two frightened small children. Haim stood protectively at the side of his sister. Angel stretched out hands clasped in prayer, pleading. A bullet passed through both her arms and she fell in a pool of her own blood. . . .

Haim seemed to have stood before the house for a long time as these memories flickered vividly on the screen of his mind. A white-haired stranger passing by noticed the look of suffering on Haim's face. 'Can I do anything for you?' he asked.

'No, no,' replied Haim, slowly returning to awareness of his surroundings.

'Perhaps memories have brought you here?' the stranger asked intuitively. Haim's silence and the sad look on his face held him.

'You are a stranger here, aren't you?' he asked.

'I lived on this street when I was a boy,' Haim replied. 'I come now from Israel.'

The stranger understood. 'There is nothing much left of the past in this town, except memories.' The stranger shook his head sadly. 'Memories, haunting memories. This very house before which you stand was built on the site of the house of a very dear friend who lived here before the war. She had always loved the Jews and went through an agony of suffering for them and with them. She lost both her arms in an effort to save a Jewish family. They all perished in the gas ovens. She survived the concentration camps and is now old and helpless in an institution in Switzerland.'

*   *   *

After he had finished recounting this story, we sat silently for quite a while.

Haim then looked lovingly at the woman beside him and

G

said, 'Angel was with us last night as we sat around the
table and I kindled the first Hanukka light with the prayer
that my father had taught me as a small boy, and our
children happily sang the Hanukka songs. We spoke of the
miracle of the light and the Lord's deliverance. And in the
children's singing were the echoes of that other singing, and
the voices of that family in Angel's cellar seemed to mingle
with ours.'

'Haim,' said Angel in faltering English, 'you forgot to
tell about the Christmas tree you prepared for me last night.
How beautiful it was with the candle on top surrounded by
the angels!'

Haim reminded us how Angel had robbed her own
Christmas tree to provide lights for the menorah in the
cellar. She looked at him lovingly and then told us how
Haim had lit the candle on top of the Christmas tree for
her. I was sure that the tears in Angel's eyes had again
shone like the stars in heaven, as love had flowed from heart
to heart.

Chapter Six

It was our second year on the Mount. One day I had been out shopping for provisions, and on my return I found the barrier across the road unlocked and a small group of men in heated discussion a little way up the road. I lifted the bar, drove the car through and lowered the bar again. I was about to turn my key in the lock when the men called to me that they would lock it.

Unusual, to say the least; the lock open and men who had a key. I called a greeting to them as I passed.

The End of Peace on Mount Zion

Some days later two men stood on our balcony, one from the Ministry of Transport, the second from the Ministry of Tourism. They were looking down at the Pope's Parking Lot on to the corrugated iron fence marking the border.

'I think this whole square should be made into a garden,' I volunteered. 'A garden of peace on Mount Zion, in the hope that one day it will be possible to extend it beyond the border.'

'But this is the only way for transport to come up to Mount Zion,' replied the man from the Transport Ministry. 'We're thinking of improving the road and making this a parking place for cars and tourist buses.'

My heart seemed to miss a beat and he must have noticed the look on my face: 'After all, we have to do all we can to encourage tourism,' he went on. 'You can't stop progress.'

'I don't think that the lack of motor transport to Mount Zion has prevented tourists from coming here,' I replied.

'On the contrary, walking up the steps they were conscious of having made a pilgrimage to a holy place.'

As we were speaking, some friends arrived at our gate to ask if they might bring their English guests up to see the view from our balcony.

Later, as we all sat together with the gentlemen from the Ministries drinking the tea specially prepared for the English visitors, one of the tourists remarked: 'In this house I feel a sense of perfect peace, even though one knows guns are probably being pointed at us this very minute.'

I looked at the man from the Ministry of Tourism. 'Do you think this peace will survive?' I asked him, 'when buses and motor cars come up here to fill the Square?'

'Maybe not,' he answered, 'but it will certainly make it easier for the tourists to get here.'

Incredulously, one of the tourists exclaimed: 'You're surely not considering allowing unrestricted traffic on Mount Zion? It'll destroy the one place in Israel which still retains some sanctity. Buses and cars up here on Mount Zion . . . it's unthinkable!'

'But let's say you were unable to walk up the steps—how would you get here?' asked the representative of tourism.

'I happen to be one of those for whom it is not easy to climb the steps,' the tourist answered. 'I've a physical disability and was compelled to take it very slowly, and the intervals of rest on the way up gave me time for reflection and contemplation—made the pilgrimage to Mount Zion more meaningful. By the time I reached the summit I somehow felt more attuned, ready for the experience awaiting me. I'd never have felt the same coming up directly by car.'

The man from the Ministry of Tourism shook his head. I suggested that for those genuinely debarred from coming to Mount Zion by physical disablement—a point he had raised—special permission to drive up the road might be granted. Nobody should be hindered from coming, but it was not necessary to open the road to the public.

But I heard the distant rumbling of the wheels of modern civilization on their way to Mount Zion, and I had already recognized that they could not be halted. It was not long before the white pegs set up by the surveyors were to be seen at intervals at the side of the road.

David Palombo, alighting from his scooter one day, said to me: 'Have you seen what is going on? This is the beginning of the end of peace on Mount Zion. Nothing will stop them now. Mount Zion will become like all other commercial tourist attractions and then it will be time for us to leave.'

The pigeons sat on the roof of the little museum, as though listening to David's words.

The Road

Tourism and transport had won the battle against the preservation of the peace and sanctity on Mount Zion.

When the clouds had unburdened themselves of the last rains of winter, what had at first been merely a disquieting sense of foreboding, grew deeper and was transformed into reality: the din and roar of bulldozers, jackhammers and heavy vehicles together with the noise of workmen had come to Mount Zion. The road was being widened and resurfaced for large tourist buses. Clouds of dust rose in the air until the leaves of the trees, washed clean by the rains, lost their sheen under this yellow pall.

All nature had responded to the call of spring, and the garden was green with life. At daybreak the silence was still broken by birdsong in praise of the new day, and a little later the voice of Ya'acov chanting his prayers on the roof of King David's Tomb was to be heard. The pigeons sat waiting on the roof of the little museum, hunched into their feathers. The sun was not far above the horizon when their friend, Obadiah, appeared with their food. Wings circled our heads and then the pigeons settled down in Garden Square as he scattered the grain. Some doves were eating out of his hand.

But Obadiah looked unhappy. The smile we had become so accustomed to was not there. He explained that when the present supply of food was finished, no more was to be bought. The Committee of Mount Zion had finally decided to stop feeding the pigeons.

The thought of Mount Zion without the flutter of wings and the cooing of doves was for me like the severing of a silver thread connecting heaven and earth. Obadiah felt that his very special mission on Mount Zion was ending.

'There'll be no need to come to Mount Zion then,' he said. 'The Doctor told me to stop working a long time ago. I'll just have to take my pension.'

He spoke as though his life was over. His wizened face seemed to shrink; his back bent even lower.

'But I'll come to see your garden sometimes,' he said.

'Don't despair, Obadiah,' I said. 'I'll buy food for the pigeons and we can even feed them together.' His eyes were misty. He turned and walked away.

All through the following months the noise and dust of the roadmaking continued. Towards the end of the summer the work was done—a good wide road for all types of transport up to Mount Zion. But the road barrier was again lowered as a battle raged between the representative authorities—religious and non-religious. I made a last appeal for the preservation of peace on Mount Zion.

The battle was fought over the closing of the road on the Sabbath. The religious were concerned only with the Sabbath. The Ministry of Tourism was concerned for the many tourists, both non-orthodox and gentile. It claimed that this was now a public road and there was no reason to close it on the Sabbath. I asked that the road be used at any time *only* for those who were unable to walk up the road or climb the steps.

The progress of the battle was reflected in the barrier across the road. Some days it was locked, some days it was open, and then one day it was removed altogether. The road was opened to all traffic, but a sign was erected at the foot of Mount Zion prohibiting the use of the road to all vehicles on the Sabbath. This very clear signpost was ignored; people merely drove right past it.

At the same time the little museum with its small display of Jewish religious objects, including a replica of the Temple, was emptied of its contents as workmen began preparing shelves and showcases to hold souvenirs for the tourist trade.

The peace and silence of Mount Zion was shattered. Noisily the cars and tourist buses climbed the hill, disgorging passengers and guides and filling Garden Square and the Pope's Parking Lot with waiting vehicles, polluting the air with petrol fumes and ruthlessly ignoring the sanctity of this Holy Hill. Guides gathered their tourist groups with loudspeakers; drivers of cars shouted for parking space; radios were left turned on in waiting buses, as were noisy air-conditioners, and the strident voices of the tourists added to the general clamour. No longer were they able to experience the sense of awe Mount Zion had previously evoked.

As I looked through my window it all seemed to be a bad dream. What forces had been allowed to take control of Mount Zion? Was this not the power which gripped the steering-wheel of modern civilization?

Then other workmen were erecting garish signboards around the souvenir shop, which greeted the visitor with: 'Welcome to Mount Zion', 'Remember your visit by taking with you a souvenir of Israeli Handicrafts', 'Jewellery, Bibles and religious articles can be purchased here', and 'We also serve cold and hot drinks and snacks'.

I remembered my first ascent up the steps to Mount Zion.

There had been very different signboards along the path. On them were written quotations from the psalms: 'Give thanks to the name of the Lord . . .', 'Pray for the peace of Jerusalem . . .', and 'The Lord is great in Zion . . .'.

* * *

The curious Arab soldiers watched from across the fence as Garden Square was turned into what closely resembled a circus.

The chanting of prayers in the synagogue on the Sabbath could no longer be heard. They were drowned by the screeching rhythms of modern dance music from the radios of waiting tourist buses. This deeply offended the religious worshippers and provoked vehement protest. Since the signboard prohibiting traffic on the Sabbath was being ignored, a strong iron chain was padlocked across the road at the foot of Mount Zion shortly before the Sabbath commenced on Friday afternoon, and was removed only at the conclusion of the Sabbath on the following evening.

Destiny

One Sabbath morning, after the chain had been put up, David Palombo brought little Paulita out into Garden Square.

'At least we have peace now for one day in the week,' he remarked. 'While I do not agree with the ways of the orthodox, I am certainly thankful for the chain across the road.'

I, too, was thankful that the peace of the Sabbath day could again be felt on Mount Zion.

But the battle continued. One Sabbath eve, the chain was broken and motor vehicles again defied the prohibition. The chain was repaired by David himself, and replaced the following Sabbath.

'Nobody,' David had said exultantly, 'will be able to break through it again.'

Destiny works in strange ways. Man may believe that he controls his life and his work, but Jeremiah says: *'O Lord, I know that the way of man is not in himself: it is not in man that walketh to direct his steps.'*

Some weeks later David learned that he had received one of the Unesco prizes for art in an international contest. He was overjoyed, particularly since the prize would enable him to have a year's study in a foreign country. He chose Japan and was beginning to make preparations for his journey. He stood at the threshold of his career as a very gifted sculptor. Israel was proud of him.

One Sabbath morning, with the chain across the road and the quiet it ensured, David and Yona were strolling in Garden Square, playing happily with Paulita. Beams of sunlight pierced the shady leaves of the trees where doves sat cooing. The members of the congregation in the little synagogue had finished morning prayers and were slowly disappearing round the bend of the road and down the hill.

David was exultantly happy—he seemed unable to contain his excitement and joy at the prospect of fulfilling a long-cherished dream—to work in Japan. In the twilight at the end of that Sabbath day, we heard the familiar sound of David starting up the motor of his scooter and speeding down the hill.

It was to be his last journey. He drove his scooter right into the chain and died of his injuries a few hours later. How it could have happened remains a mystery to this day, for David had the key to the padlock in his pocket.

His tragic death left its mark on Mount Zion: the road was never again closed, and the peace we had known before the new road was opened went forever. Only in the very early hours of dawn were we aware of its fleeting presence.

Chapter Seven

1967: The Approach of War

All through the month of May 1967, the storm clouds darkened on the horizon. Egypt was massing troops on the border and building up a formidable military force ready for attack; Israel was preparing to defend herself. Each day the situation became more serious. All our able-bodied men were being called up. The roads were filled with military vehicles carrying soldiers and equipment.

Many more soldiers were being posted to Mount Zion and every corner was inspected as plans for its defence went ahead. It was dangerous to linger near the border at night. The local commander of the military post and some of his soldiers dropped in often for a drink and a chat. Also our Nahal soldiers were frequently with us. We shared the dangers lurking in the darkness, our tomorrow held in the closed hand of the unknown.

The atmosphere was charged with tense expectancy, and a fear which we hid or tried to reject. An unusual quality had been added to our lives. Conversations, although bravely optimistic, were often tinged with anxiety. Everything seemed to be under a spell. The dark clouds cast dark shadows and the shadows formed the dreaded word—War!

War was threatening our beloved land. Was war poking its ugly finger into every home and opening its grasping hand? Was it really possible that we were on the brink of war? It all seemed so unreal, like some nightmarish dream. But homes were being emptied of sons, fathers, brothers, husbands, who one by one had been called to military duty. The whole of Jerusalem seemed to be on the alert.

Through my window I saw great lorries spilling sand into Garden Square, where buses were now no longer allowed. Other vehicles were depositing hundreds of small sacks beside the mound of sand. Each day schoolchildren and other youths were filling the sandbags and piling them up ready to be used to reinforce the windows of the military post, the Nahal quarters, and to protect other buildings on Mount Zion. The feeling of the imminence of war intensified each day, and when the United Nations forces left Gaza at Nasser's request we realized the seriousness of our position.

Raymond, a Christian friend from England who had been with us for six weeks, was due to return to London on June 15th. We tried to persuade him to leave before the trouble started.

'It would be wiser for you to return now,' we told him. 'Your family is dependent on you and you should also consider your responsibility to your job.'

He was silent and thoughtful.

'War could start at any moment,' I continued, 'and no one can predict how long it will be before you can return to your family or what might happen under such circumstances.'

Raymond was silent for a long time before he replied: 'I'd never feel at peace with myself if I left Israel now.' And again he paused, 'I came here because I felt I had a command from above to come to Jerusalem; I'll wait now for the command to leave. My family will understand.'

His decision was made. The next day he received a letter from his family telling him not to leave Mount Zion at this time, that they would manage without him if he could not return and they too would feel that they were sharing in Israel's destiny.

Thursday, June 1st

The month began with a great movement of people: citizens of other nations who had been advised to leave and Israelis abroad who were hurrying to return.

Our friend Gilbert, the reform rabbi in the States, had been in Israel with his family for two months. He came to say goodbye to us. He was taking his family back home.

'The situation is very serious,' he said. 'It seems that war is inevitable.'

He was very depressed. 'And when all the Arab countries around us come against us intending to destroy us completely, what chance have we got?' Gloom and pessimism enveloped him in a dark aura.

'I also believe that war is on our doorstep,' I replied, 'but I would ask what chance the Arabs have when they come to fight against Israel.'

'But look at their strength and their numbers, and we are surrounded by them.'

'Do you think, Gilbert,' Albert broke in, 'that we've been brought back to our land after nearly two thousand years of dispersion, only to be destroyed by our neighbours? I cannot believe that God gave us a State of Israel for that purpose.'

'I agree with Albert,' I said. 'You know the Biblical history of our people. You know what befalls the enemies of Israel who attempt to foil the plan of God.'

Gilbert was not comforted. I reminded him of the Bible account: '*When the Syrians came in great strength against Israel and the servant of Elisha, the man of God, saw the great host that came by night and compassed the city about, he said to Elisha, "alas my master how shall we do?"* I can imagine that he felt as depressed as you do today. But Elisha answered, "*Fear not, they that be with us are more than they that be with them*". I believe that at this time also, when we are compelled to meet the enemy in battle, those hosts of the Lord will be on our side, with our armies, and we need have no fear. We will have the victory and see some great miracles.'

'You are an incorrigible dreamer,' Gilbert replied. 'You live in a visionary world of miracles, but I see facts and realities—and you cannot ignore facts.'

'Perhaps my dreams and visions are the realities,' I answered, 'and your facts and realities are but edifices erected on crumbling foundations.'

As he was about to leave, a commander and some of his men came to tell us that we should prepare to be evacuated from Mount Zion at once. 'You can't possibly remain in this house exposed to the enemy on nearly all sides. Look down at those Arab soldiers right now.'

'We do not want to leave Mount Zion,' I said.

'But you've no protection here and the enemy is only a few yards away. Go to the city, where there are shelters.'

Albert said quietly: 'We have the best protection and the best shelter.'

'Where?' asked the commander in surprise.

Albert looked upwards. 'Above us,' he replied. 'The Almighty can protect us here just as well as in the city.'

'I do not think that is very sensible,' the commander said, and began to look around the house for a safe place. Finally he said: 'You can't stay in this house. If you're foolish enough to remain on Mount Zion and the shooting starts, you must go into the Palombo Gallery at the back of the house. That at least affords a little protection.'

Gilbert embraced us in silence and left.

Yona, living above the gallery, was also very reluctant to leave Mount Zion. But she had been persuaded to go and stay with relatives in the city for little Paulita's sake.

That night we received a cable from Christian friends in Germany—a mother and her married son—saying they would be arriving the following day. This astonished us. Why come at this dangerous time? Did they not know the seriousness of the situation? We cabled back: 'Unwise to come now.'

Friday, June 2nd

Tired after a difficult journey, but radiating love and thankfulness, our friends arrived. They embraced us warmly:

'Your cable could not stop us. We just wanted to clasp your hands in friendship and assure you of our unity and prayers for you and for Israel when you face the trials of war.'

'Didn't you know that war might start at any moment and you may not be able to return to your family?'

'Yes,' they replied, 'but we were prepared to take this risk if we could only get on a plane.'

Albert and I were overwhelmed.

'There was only one plane from Zürich. They told us that Lydda airport was closed to all but military planes, and this was only taking personnel back to Israel. They thought we were quite mad even to think of going to Israel.'

'Then how did you get here?'

'God helped us and finally they consented to take us. We are so thankful that we can see you again and stand on the soil of Israel at this time. We can be with you for twenty-four hours. A plane will take us back tomorrow night.'

Those twenty-four hours were filled with constant reminders of the possible ordeal which would confront us at any moment. Soldiers came in to see which windows needed the protection of sandbags.

'I would rather not have any sandbags,' I said.

'Then get paper strips to paste on all the windows,' they replied. They brought me rolls of narrow strips of paper to protect the glass from splintering.

'I won't need them.' I said.

'Why not?'

'Because I believe in other protection.'

We brought up some camp beds from the cellar. Soldiers were in and out of the house all day. 'You must not think of sleeping in this house if trouble starts,' we were told. 'Take the beds into the Palombo Gallery now.' We folded up the beds and sleeping-bags and took them into the gallery.

Sabbath Eve, June 2nd

At sunset Albert joined the usual little congregation assembled on the roof of King David's Tomb for the Sabbath evening service—the faithful Rabbi Uri and some of the Nahal boys and two other soldiers.

Rabbi Uri for the first time seemed depressed and, as he stood facing the Temple area in the Old City, said to Albert: 'Again we have to fight our enemies. When will they leave us in peace?'

Albert answered cheerfully: 'Next Friday we'll all be at the Wailing Wall.'

The soldiers smiled at this incredible thought.

'May the Almighty grant us this,' Rabbi Uri said sadly. 'How long have we waited for that day, and how much longer must we wait?' His voice was like a cry ascending to the Creator.

The Sabbath, June 3rd

Twenty-four hours had passed and the time had come for our friends to depart. They had brought us joy and given us encouragement. The spirit of love and friendship remained the only reality which could not be shaken by events. It was like a deep well from which one could draw strength to face the unknown.

We were relieved to see their plane airborne. It could so easily have been otherwise. What experiences lay before us before we would clasp their hands again?

Sunday, June 4th

Danny, our Nahal friend, came in for a few minutes. He was in full battle-dress: rifle over his shoulder and helmet covered with leafy twigs. 'We have to be prepared for attack by the Jordanians at any moment,' he said. 'Many people do not believe that Jordan will fight us. Israel has

told King Hussein that we will not do anything to them if
they do not attack us. It may be quiet here on our border.
In any case take provisions and all that you need into the
gallery. It's better that you should be there and not in the
house in case of any surprises.' Another Nahal soldier came
to call him and they walked away deep in serious conversation.

Monday, June 5th

At daybreak, as usual, I scattered the grain for the pigeons
and doves. Some were eating out of my hand as the sparrows
waited for the gleanings. Tamar, at a safe distance behind a
closed gate, watched with interest. There seemed to be
fewer birds than usual this morning—as though they had
sensed the danger and had stayed away.

This peaceful hour on Mount Zion at sunrise seemed, on
this morning of June 5th, to have a special significance. The
rising sun, the lightening sky, the fluttering wings, the birdsong and the fragrance of flowers were all as usual, evidence
of heavenly powers, gifts of God to the earth and to mankind, regardless of good or evil.

I walked around the garden where the tall white madonna
lilies, in all their purity, shyly hung their heads and mingled
their perfume with that of the gay frilly blossoms of the
sweet peas covering the wall behind them.

The pink, blue and white larkspur, tall and heavy with
blossom, mingled round the lemon tree already hung with
its ripe yellow fruit. Different coloured petunias and ver-
benas were massed to make a carpet between the taller
flowers. Hibiscus buds were turning scarlet and the branches
of the oleanders were bent low with their profusion of
sweet-scented pink blossoms.

I looked at the jacaranda tree, in its exposed position. It
had grown tall and strong, its young branches already
giving shade to the hot corner. If it survived the war, it
would flower the following year.

The garden seemed to be singing with joy with each plant displaying its colour and form. I looked over the stone wall of the garden to the corrugated iron fence on the border, and behind it the fortified Jordanian military post. I saw some of our soldiers walking up the hill and military vehicles were all around our military post.

The joy of the garden remained enclosed in its surrounding wall. Beyond the wall the stillness was heavy with foreboding. The quiet was broken by the footsteps of soldiers passing the house and entering the Gallery building.

Everything, everybody seemed to be waiting . . . waiting . . . waiting for that dreaded thing which meant death, destruction and suffering, fascinated by its evil spell, its magic which could drive men to the depths of cruelty and horror and could also raise them to heights of self-sacrifice, brotherly love and endurance.

I went indoors with a heavy heart, but I could also feel waves of excitement passing through me. Were we on the threshold of another chapter of our history, another step forward in the plan of God for Israel, in whose destiny the whole world was involved?

Albert and Raymond were preparing to go into the city. Albert had a matter to attend to at the Foreign Ministry. They would also look for more provisions. We had been told to collect a store of food to last at least two weeks. The shops had already been emptied of most essential food-stuffs days ago.

As I watched our car with Albert, Raymond and Tamar disappearing down the hill I saw Yona approaching.

'What have you come for?' I asked in surprise.

'I forgot some important things,' she answered. 'But I'll not be here long. Paulita and I are well set-up in town. I would much rather be here with you,' she continued, 'but of course I could not stay here with Paulita.'

Yona went into the Gallery and I began to sort out a few provisions to take into the Gallery—just in case. . . . While

H

I was packing a box with necessaries, Danny came in and asked: 'Did you hear the news on the radio?'

'No,' I replied. I looked at him intently. 'Is it war?'

He nodded his head. 'It has started in Gaza. Where is Albert?'

'In town with Raymond and Tamar.'

He looked worried. 'Everyone was told to go into their shelters and remain there. The battle may start also in Jerusalem.' He ran off to his post, calling to me to go into the Gallery.

'It has started!' Danny's words rang in my ears. How many young men, Israeli and Egyptian, had already lost their lives? It had started: death, suffering, agony, destruction.

I thought of Jeremiah's words: '*It is not in man that walketh to direct his steps.*' His steps were directed by the powers which he served and obeyed—the power which gave life and peace or the power which led man to death and destruction. The discernment of these hidden powers is the greatest wisdom we can have, for darkness sometimes appears in the garb of light.

War on Mount Zion

As I was finishing packing the box of provisions I looked out to Garden Square. There was nobody to be seen. A stillness had overtaken Mount Zion. A quietness from which peace had fled, leaving only a silence, a silence breathless and fearsome, awaiting its death. How long would it be?

As I reached the foot of the stairs with the box of provisions the silence died. Suddenly the noise of machine-gun shells and rifle fire rent the air. Bullets were flying in all directions and as they hit the walls I knew that I must leave everything and make a dash for the Gallery. Remembering a pot of potatoes cooking on the stove I ran upstairs to turn off the gas, trying to avoid the windows.

Then I made a dive for the open door of the Gallery which faced the Jordanian soldiers and above which our soldiers were returning fire. Yona stood inside with her case packed ready to leave. Her thoughts were centred on Paulita and how she could get to her. We heard the whizz of shells going over into the City. I wondered where Albert and Raymond were and hoped that they were not exposed to the bullets and shells.

We spoke little as we stood listening. Then we heard a car stop not far from our door and moments later two men rushed into the Gallery—two priests, members of one of the churches on Mount Zion. We looked at them in astonishment.

'How did you get here?' we asked.

'We were on our way from the city when it started. There was nothing to be done but continue. Bullets were flying all around us, but, as you see, we have arrived safely.' They could not go further than the Gallery—the path to the church was fraught with too many dangers. So they stayed with us.

The noise was deafening and continuous. It sounded as if every bullet hit the wall of the Gallery and every explosion was outside our door. The play of sound was very mis-leading.

Yona paced the floor, deeply troubled: 'I left Paulita in the kindergarten,' she said, 'and I was to call for her at lunchtime. She will be so frightened. I must get to her somehow.'

We tried to comfort her and reassure her with the thought that all the children would be in a shelter and well cared for. I had my own anxieties about Albert and Raymond.

Half an hour passed and the ring of the telephone could scarcely be heard above the din of the battle. With great relief I heard Albert's voice on the line.

'We got caught at the Ministry,' he said. 'I am in a shelter here, but I do not know where Raymond is and we left

Tamar in the car. The shelling is fairly heavy, but do not worry and keep in a safe place.'

Later there was another phone call from Albert: 'We are now all together in a shelter at the King's Hotel. Tamar has survived the shock of the noise. We'll be staying here while the shelling of the City goes on.' I was greatly relieved.

A call also came through some time later from Yona's friends: 'Paulita is with us in a shelter. All is well, we will take good care of her.' How deeply thankful we were for the phone.

There was no lull in the fighting that whole day. Shots were being fired from above the Gallery and from all the posts around us. Also the bullets and shells were coming from the other side of Mount Zion. It was a great battle. Jerusalem—City of Peace—heralding by its name its ultimate destiny, was once again being lashed by the enemies of peace.

At dusk, in a short interval in which the firing seemed less intense, I ran across to the house and grabbed the box of provisions which I had left near the door in the morning. We had not eaten the whole day nor had anything to drink. But that night we had some biscuits and cheese and with a little water we made some coffee. Later I could again run into the house and get some more provisions.

Yona was getting restless. 'Now that it is dark,' she said, 'I will try to walk down the steps into the City. I must get to Paulita.'

'That would be suicide,' we told her as we listened to the fury of the battle.

'I think I could find the secret tunnel under Mount Zion, used by the soldiers,' she continued. We sought to calm her and dissuade her from endangering her life.

We began to look for the safest place to put up our beds. There was a space between two large stone pillars, which would give us protection from the bullets and flying shrapnel that could come through the open ironwork of the doors.

The four beds fitted into this space without an inch between them. The two priests chose to be pressed against the stone pillars; Yona and I lay side by side on the beds in the middle. We tried to sleep but it was impossible. The battle for Jerusalem raged all night with unabated fury. Added to the deafening noise of shells and bullets was the roar of war planes flying over Mount Zion in waves with such speed and power, scooping up every other sound in their path and then casting it all back to earth with such a thunderous roar that it seemed as if our ears would be shattered.

We listened to all the firing on Mount Zion, not knowing which was from our side and which from the Arabs, and because every shot and explosion always sounded as if it was destined for our wall, I imagined that little would be left of our house. Perhaps it had already been reduced to greater ruin than when we first saw it.

We had the radio on all the time. During that terrible night, in the midst of all the shooting, there were strains of most wonderful music which mingled with, or was sporadically drowned out by the gun and shell fire. Never was music so sweet or so soothing to our nerves. . . .

We heard that the United Nations Headquarters had been taken by the Jordanians; not much later it was in Israeli hands. There was fierce fighting to the right of us, on the hill of Abu Tor, also on Mount Scopus and in the Mea Shearim quarter. Then we heard that four hundred Egyptian planes had been destroyed. We looked at one another.

'That is surely impossible,' someone remarked.

'They must have made a mistake in the announcement,' said Yona. 'Perhaps they meant forty.'

But there had been no mistake in the announcement.

During the night Yona and I had to brave the bullets and flying shrapnel and go upstairs. The toilet was situated on the open roof, next to the room where our soldiers were shooting from behind sand-bagged windows. On this open roof, the whizzing of shells and bullets and the noise of their hitting the stones seemed so unreal that we did not fully comprehend the danger in which we stood. A great blaze in front of the Dormition Church lit up the whole area. Then, suddenly, the dome of the Church went up in flames. . . .

We crept along the wall to the stone steps and as we descended into the Gallery, flares were falling, filling the passageway between our house and the Gallery with a flood of light. How beautiful the tracery of the ironwork of the doors looked, with their bits of pointed and curled iron darkly silhouetted against the light, like the leaves of trees against a bright sun.

We all returned to our beds, lying very quiet and still hoping we would be able to sleep a little, but before long we had our own battle to fight—with the sand flies! Those tiny almost invisible insects which torment humans living on the edge of the desert, and include Mount Zion in their sphere of action.

They came in full strength, without screens on the windows to hinder them. Their attack nearly drove us crazy. The minute injections which they left under the skin in place of the blood they had extracted covered every part of our exposed skin with swelling red lumps and an itch which never abated. Nobody could lie still any longer.

In the early hours of the morning there was a slight lull and some of our Nahal boys came in to see if we were all right and to let us know that all was well with them. How relieved we were to see them! They could only stay a few moments. The commander came down from the room on the roof and told us our boys were encircling the Old City.

When it was daylight one of our companions accompanied me into the house. Everything looked all right downstairs, but we did not go upstairs as bullets were flying all the time. We grabbed a few more provisions and a paraffin stove and ran back into the Gallery. The lull did not last long. Suddenly the shooting started in earnest again. Nobody was in sight.

Tuesday, June 6th

A day we shall never forget. All day, without a stop, bullets and shells were flying and exploding. Always the noise seemed to be just outside the Gallery. We were in touch with Albert and Raymond from time to time by phone; they were still at the King's Hotel in a shelter and all was well with them. Paulita was also in a safe place. Jerusalem was being heavily shelled, but the news was encouraging.

Israeli forces were occupying so many places, making such rapid progress, it was hard to believe.

The battle continued all day, and that day we did not see anyone and were wondering what was happening to our boys and all the soldiers here on Mount Zion. And what was happening to our house? Were the Jordanians on our border making any advance? We knew only too well how close they were. We had some provisions to eat and with a little paraffin we could boil water and have a hot drink, but we could not move out of the Gallery the whole day and going upstairs was always a great risk.

Brother Daniel, one of our companions, spent much time reading from his prayer book, and Father Samuel kept on trying to get different stations on his transistor. Conversation did not flow easily, we each had our secret thoughts and the incessant noise outside kept us quiet.

Father Samuel, his transistor held to his ear, suddenly grew very intent, listening. By coincidence he had tuned to a station broadcasting in Arabic, which he understood. When it was finished he said simply: 'King Hussein giving orders to his soldiers: "Kill every Jew you encounter, kill them with your guns, your hands, your feet, your teeth—only kill them".'

At nightfall the shooting died down a little. The Commander came down looking exhausted and preoccupied. We made some coffee for him and he told us our progress had been amazing. The Arab military post opposite us had been conquered and also other surrounding Jordanian posts; only one of his men had been slightly wounded and the others were perfectly all right.

He was a soldier in the regular army, a man with his two feet planted firmly on the ground, his hands trained to use a gun, and his personality shaped to lead his men.

'I have had some strange experiences today,' he said quietly. His thoughts seemed to be travelling in unaccustomed paths. 'Every bullet we fired struck its target. Whatever we did, succeeded. We were amazed to see how quickly the Arabs evacuated their posts.'

He sat sprawling on a chair, his long legs stretched out, his broad shoulders drooped slightly as he relaxed for the few minutes while he drank his coffee. He was very silent, and then as though speaking to himself, he said: 'I cannot believe the things I did today. It was as though someone else was commanding. . . .' Then he returned to his men upstairs.

Later Danny and Efraim came across the courtyard from their post on the border, braving the intermittent shooting. Their hands were blackened by gunpowder and sweaty and their boyish faces were smeared and showing signs of strain and exhaustion.

'Everything is all right,' they assured us. We thanked God.

'Stay here and have some coffee,' we suggested.

'No, we must return at once. We only wanted to know how things were with you.'

They bent their helmeted heads low as they felt their way along the walls on their way back. That day had changed them from carefree boys to responsible men—defenders of Mount Zion.

We prepared to settle for the night. Yona insisted on

going upstairs to find some mosquito nets so that we could have some relief from the sand flies. Father Samuel and I lay side by side under one net and Brother Daniel and Yona under another. We were as close together as it was possible to be on account of limited space. I laughed inwardly as I found myself in this situation with Yona and the two priests. It seemed so funny and I thought how war can change the normal rules and customs of life!

We were tucked in our sleeping-bags, and by midnight were so exhausted that we were no longer disturbed by the infernal noise and we all went to sleep. An hour later we were awakened by a very loud explosion in our vicinity.

'That was very close,' said Yona.

Perhaps our house was shelled, I thought, wondering how much damage had been done.

We fell asleep again until dawn. Then we made a hot drink and heard the most fantastic news. Most of the posts around Jerusalem had been taken and it seemed that soon we would be in the Old City. We just couldn't believe it.

Wednesday, June 7th

As the first rays of light uncovered the darkness of that terrible night, the shooting died down and there was much movement in Garden Square. It was suddenly filled with soldiers and trucks, and by the time the sun had risen a little above the horizon the shooting had almost stopped.

We went outside for the first time. I looked at our house —it was still standing intact. I rushed upstairs. Everything was covered with a thick layer of dust and dirt which had fallen from the ceiling with every explosion, but I could not see any damage, not even a broken window. I was astonished. Then I went into our bedroom and saw holes in the wall. Six bullets had left as many holes in the wall above the wardrobe; they had pierced the window, making six holes in the curtains. No other damage.

'But where could that loud explosion have been?' I was thinking, when Brother Daniel came to tell us that a shell had exploded in the house belonging to the Church next to the Gallery.

In addition to this, the Church dome had suffered, and a few more holes had appeared in the walls of the military post. We could not see any other damage on the whole of Mount Zion. Where had all the bullets and shells landed during those two days and nights of constant battle? It really was a miracle. Mount Zion seemed to have been specially protected. I remembered the Commander's words: 'It was as though someone else was commanding. . . .'

Yona and I talked to the fifty or so soldiers who filled the Square. They were very tired, but the time had not yet come for them to rest. We made them strong Turkish coffee, and never was coffee more appreciated or of greater help. They had not had a hot drink for almost thirty hours—hours of harrowing experiences, and difficulty, still lay ahead of them in the Old City.

There was an atmosphere of excitement among them all. Something portentous was going to happen. Then the Commander of the unit said to me: 'We are now going into the Old City through this border on Mount Zion to meet up with our boys who are entering the City through other gates. But we have no flag with us, and we *must* have a flag.' He looked at me questioningly. 'Can you help us? There is no time to lose.'

'Come with me,' I answered, and rushed upstairs. I took a sheet out of the linen cupboard and remembered that I had a new tube of blue watercolour paint.

We spread the white sheet on the kitchen table and excitedly, with the watercolour running, painted on the Star of David. My heart beat very fast as we attached and then rolled up the flag on a stick from the garden and gave it to the Commander.

We watched the jeeps and half-tracks, filled with soldiers,

descending the hill and crossing the border into the Old City. We wondered what would happen to those boys and our hurriedly improvised flag. Many thoughts passed through my mind. The flag of the State of Israel was going from this house into the Old City. Would it be the flag of victory hoisted on the walls of Jerusalem when the City was liberated?

The shooting started again. There was hard fighting in the streets and blood flowed in the narrow alleyways of the Old City. A high price was being paid in human lives and suffering in order to break down the walls of hatred and division.

There are moments on the road of destiny which inspire fanciful thoughts, perhaps even prophetic thoughts. I looked into the future, the promised future, when the State of Israel would become the Kingdom of Israel, the Kingdom of peace, the Kingdom of God on earth with the Messiah ruling on the throne of David, and bringing peace to all the world.

The flag of the State of Israel had been made on Mount Zion at this hour of destiny. Could it be that the flag of the Kingdom of Israel would also be made here? It would be hoisted high on Mount Zion for all the world to see, a time of great rejoicing when 'the Lord of hosts shall reign in Mount Zion and in Jerusalem—gloriously'.

Later in the morning there was a silence, a strange silence, broken only by occasional shots from snipers and the frenzied voice of a demented man crying loudly in the Old City. The silence became so impelling it seemed to enter into the soul; I felt that I was holding my breath on the brink of eternity. Then the sound of a trumpet could be heard, the long blast of the ram's horn—the shofar—shattering the silence. The battle for Jerusalem was over. Rabbi Goren, the army chaplain, was blowing the shofar at the Wailing Wall, the wall of the Temple, and we could hear him singing the prayers.

At that moment all Israel was pouring out its heart in prayers. For the first time for nearly two thousand years, independent Jews were again in the City of David, at the Temple Wall, freed of its enemies. I remembered the time when Jews had stood praying at that Wall and had been stabbed in the back as they prayed.

Everybody wept for joy that morning. Even soldiers who were never in any way religious were stirred to the depths of their being and acknowledged the miracle from God. Who could have believed that only two days after fighting began we would be in the Old City again? God had shown His power in Israel for all the world to see.

During the next few hours hundreds of soldiers were sent up to Mount Zion. For two days it became a military camp. Units were sent from here to different places and were continually being replaced. It was a military camp in action. Cooks were preparing the food and men were lying and resting on every available space on the ground.

In the afternoon Yona was allowed to go to Paulita and it was possible for Albert and Raymond to return to Mount Zion. I ran to meet the car bringing them up the hill, our own car—completely undamaged.

How happy and thankful we were to be together again —unharmed. Tamar also seemed glad to be back. It was strange that we had been separated for those two hard days and nights, but that too had been the hand of Providence. However hard it had been in the city it was harder here and Tamar would never have survived, as any sound resembling a shot had always sent her into a frenzy of fear, and I would have had to use the tablets that had been given by the vet to put her to sleep in such an emergency.

Albert and Raymond told of their experiences and narrow escapes during the shelling of the city, but most of the time they had been safe in shelters.

Albert was quiet with emotion, 'Imagine the flag of

Israel on the walls of the Old City of Jerusalem after nearly two thousand years!'

'I noticed that the flag flying on David's Tower did not appear to be the usual printed flag. It looked more like a home-made one!' Raymond remarked.

My heart beat a little faster as he spoke and then I told them the story of the flag made so hurriedly on the kitchen table at Ha-Ohel—the flag destined to mark another milestone in Jewish history. How many other flags had been hoisted there since it was first a city of the Jews! How much suffering and persecution the Jews had endured under those flags since the time of King David's reign!

When we came back to the house and saw the mess that had to be cleared up, we thought at first that we would have to sleep in the Gallery. Yet with a special effort we were able to eat together in our own kitchen once more, and sleep in our own beds. It was almost impossible to grasp the fact that only two days had passed and the battle for Jerusalem was over.

However, the war had not yet ended and we listened intently to the news coming over the radio. We heard that Jericho was in our hands, and later, Hebron and Bethlehem, Ramallah and all the surrounding towns and villages. We were quite dazed. It seemed so incredible.

During the night we heard the soldiers singing as they sat around their camp fires. But intermittent shots from hidden snipers in the Old City continued. We were all exhausted, more from emotion than anything else, when we fell asleep in our own beds. . . .

Thursday, June 8th

The sun was beginning to give light to another day. I looked out of my window and saw the soldiers—exhausted —asleep on the ground. It was a strange sight in the Pope's Parking Lot and Garden Square. Gradually they stirred to life and the cooks outside our front gate began to prepare their breakfast. Then the day started for us in the house.

They wanted only two things: the telephone and water. Because of damage to the water pipes on Mount Zion they were without water, and we refilled their water bottles until our own supplies ran out. But, what they wanted most of all was to be allowed to use the telephone. Through most of the day they waited in an endless queue, it seemed, to use it for some had been unable to contact their families for a fortnight. The conversations made dents in one's soul. A young man spoke to his wife; she had heard that he had been killed and was in the midst of the seven days of mourning for her dead. He could not make her understand that he was still alive. Again and again he said: 'It is Joseph speaking—your husband. I am alive, I am alive. Don't you understand? I am alive and speaking to you from Mount Zion! Soon I'll be back.' Then he spoke to his little children. His face was set to hide his emotion.

An older man spoke to his father: 'Abba, Abba (father), I've seen our old home in the Old City where they dragged you out and took you prisoner twenty years ago. We will go back to our old home, Abba. I will take you there . . .' Tears trickled down his face. He pulled a key from his pocket and said to me: 'This is the key of our old home. I have kept it for twenty years. My mother gave it to me when she and other women with young children were allowed to go into the new Jerusalem before they burned the houses and synagogues in the Jewish Quarter of the Old City. I always believed I would find the house one day and took the key with me into battle. Our house escaped the flames. The key still fits.'

Another young blue-eyed soldier, not more than nineteen, spoke to his anxious mother who had not heard from him for two weeks. Fathers talking to their children, husbands to their wives, sons to their parents. It was hard to get them away from the telephone. These men had come through great dangers. Some told of comrades killed or wounded at their side.

It was an emotional day. So much joy, so much tragedy and such a consciousness of having experienced a miracle. Even those who had no religious beliefs at all had to acknowledge that something had happened which was beyond their power alone. They had all fought valiantly and were prepared to sacrifice their lives, but they knew that this was not all that had given them the victory.

Everyone seemed to be saying with the Commander of Mount Zion: 'It was as though someone else was commanding. . . .' In fact, one religious soldier said: 'I hope that our people will not forget that God has given us this victory.' His words reminded me of the time of the Siege of Jerusalem in 1948. Then, too, a wave of religious fervour swept through the people.

'Yes,' I answered, 'we hope that this experience will strengthen the faith of our people and bring a deeper realization of the fact that when Israel fights her battles there are also "the armies of God" fighting with her.'

'That was always true,' replied the soldier, 'just as He fights for us now.'

Friday, June 9th

In the first pale light of dawn I looked out of my window and saw intense action among the soldiers: some coming, some going. Then I learned that Egypt had accepted the United Nations cease fire. The war in Sinai was over.

A new sound drew me to my window. A large bulldozer was noisily climbing the hill. I watched it turn clumsily to face the corrugated iron fence which marked the border, marred the beauty of the landscape and was a constant reminder of the divided Jerusalem. How intensely I had always wished it could be removed!

The bulldozer was in position, its motor full on. I watched, excited and almost breathless. With a roar and a rattle I saw it break through the fence, wrenching it apart and crushing it under its wheels. Then with an added roar of power, it approached the stone building of the Jordanian military post behind the fence near our house. Nothing could stop its advance. As it passed, broken walls and mounds of scattered stones and débris were all that was left. But the great majestic trees which had shielded it from view also lay prostrate in the dust. The border had disappeared and a new road was being made. After little more than an hour of continuous work with the bulldozer a small part of the way was cleared and I saw a car coming through from the Old City. . . . It was hard to grasp the significance of this—free passage from the Old City to the New: a safe and free road from Mount Zion to the Wall— all barriers down. It was only five days since the war started!

There were occasional shots from snipers in the vicinity and the sound of mines exploding. Some anxious to find a way into the Old City, had walked in forbidden areas and many were injured by mines or snipers. It was still dangerous to move freely.

Our telephone was ringing continuously—friends enquiring how we were. Some walked up the steps to see for themselves that everything was all right, for it was not yet permitted to use the road. So many good friends. . . .

Our great problem was water—the supply was very low and we only had a trickle of water in the garden for use in the house. The poor garden was very parched but was doing its best to survive. The soldiers still came to the telephone, but most of them were now leaving Mount Zion and were being posted elsewhere. Meanwhile, we were trying to clean up the house.

At midday we were allowed to use the car to go into town. I had expected to see much damage in the city as a result of those two days of shelling, but I found no more than an occasional wall with some stones knocked out and a few broken windows. Even in the centre of the city everything seemed to be going on normally. I had heard that the Knesset museum and university had been hit, but was told that very little damage had been done. It was all part of the miracle.

Shops were open and business was as usual—and only five days after the war had begun.... We did some shopping, collected letters and cables from anxious relatives and friends, then returned home to prepare for the Sabbath.

By the evening of Saturday, June 10th, when the Syrians agreed to a cease fire, the Six Day War was over.

Chapter Eight

This was the Sabbath eve of June 9th. It was only a week before that Albert had said jokingly, but prophetically, 'Next Friday we will all go to the Wailing Wall for our service.' Then, we had smiled at so fantastic a hope.

Now, a week later, five days since the commencement of the war, Danny came to us and said: 'We are going to the Wall tonight for our service and we'll take you with us.'

'But nobody is allowed there yet,' I answered in surprise. 'It's all right if you come with us.'

Albert and I looked at each other wordlessly. We could not believe it possible. Then Albert said excitedly: 'I must find Rabbi Uri. I promised him last week that we would go to the Wall this Sabbath.' We also contacted another friend, a Rabbi, who had been trying unsuccessfully to go to the Wall.

The Wall

An hour before the Sabbath began, our little group gathered outside our gate in preparation for the precarious walk down to the Wall. A stranger managed to attach himself to us in his eagerness to get there too. He was dressed in a long, black satin coat and a large fur-brimmed hat, under which his long, well-groomed side curls almost touched his shoulders. He was a member of the ultra-orthodox community of Mea Shearim. His thick brown beard could not hide the youthfulness of his face.

Our Nahal boys were still in full battledress, with their Uzis hanging over their shoulders. Soon the stranger and the soldiers were in heated argument. The stranger insisted that the boys leave their guns behind as it was forbidden to carry anything on the Sabbath.

'If we don't carry our guns, you can't go to the Wall,' one remarked. 'We are soldiers on duty and we mustn't move a step without our guns.'

Just at that moment we heard shots from the direction in which we were to go. The stranger continued to argue and stress his point, and so we left him to his expounding of the Law, and went on our way, led by the soldiers, their guns on their shoulders. The stranger had a personal problem to solve. He did not come with us. . . .

It was not yet possible to use the clearing made by the bulldozer. We walked round to the side of the Nahal post; broken stone steps covered with rusty barbed wire led down to the road on the other side of what had been the border.

It was quite a difficult descent, but our boys helped us very lovingly over the broken stones, removing the barbed wire in our path. We followed a narrow road which curved behind an abandoned but well-established Jordanian military camp with its substantial tents and supplies of equipment. I realized then how close they had been to our house on Mount Zion!

The light was beginning to fade and we had to go down more steps darkened by the dense foliage of overhanging trees. Then we found ourselves on the road, facing the Church of St Peter in Gallicanty. The little stone houses of Silwan on the hill rising behind it were now as close as we had always seen them through our binoculars.

We stood on territory which had been forbidden to us for twenty-two years. The Old City walls, above which rose the domes and minarets of the mosques built on the Temple area, seen until now always from a distance, were suddenly so close, so very close, and we were walking towards them.

It was surely a dream, a marvellous dream, and this must be the waking moment when one strives to hold on to the

I*

vision and bring it into conscious life before it is lost. But was it a dream? I looked at Albert, Raymond, the Rabbis and our soldiers with their guns, walking protectively before us, behind us and on either side of us. A little procession of awakening dreamers, walking slowly down the road where not a living soul could be seen.

Wrecked and abandoned cars were like corpses on the roadside. Everything was silent, so silent that our footsteps seemed to have unending echoes, echoes of the footsteps of all the House of Israel walking to the Wall—to the Temple.

We passed a few Arab houses as we approached the Dung Gate, and from each house a piece of white cloth hung from a pole. From the balcony of one house an Arab man and woman stood watching us. The first sign of life. We waved to them and called 'Shalom!' They returned the greeting, smiling. It was our first greeting of peace to our Arab neighbours! This, too, was part of the dream. . . .

We passed through the Dung Gate into the Old City. We were now within its walls, walking through the winding, narrow cobbled streets lined with old houses. At the end of the road was an opening in a stone wall revealing part of the greater wall a few yards behind it, a wall built of stones so huge that the others seemed like pebbles by comparison.

Still on the edge of a dream we entered the opening and with hearts deeply stirred, stood in the small space before those great stones of the Wailing Wall. The Wall with its power of conjuring up visions of Solomon's Temple in all its glory.

Since the time of the destruction of the Temple and the dispersal of the Jews this Wall had received into itself tears of sorrow and mourning, cries of anguish and supplication, prayers and pleas to the Almighty for mercy and restoration, flowing from Jewish hearts all over the world.

The bond of the Jew with Jerusalem and the Temple could never be severed. The silver cord which carried the cries, prayers, hopes and faith of the Jews towards this place could not be touched by suffering, persecution or death. The world with all its powers could not destroy it. And now, the enemies with all their might and determination had not succeeded in preventing the return of the Jewish People to the Wall.

We did not speak of conquest in this war. Our victory had been the return to the Wall.

I remembered my first glimpse of this Wall in 1946. Nothing had changed. I remembered how all the cracks and crevices in the stones had been filled with small rolled pieces of paper on which were written petitions to the Creator of those praying before it, in the belief that here, as in the Temple, they were nearer to God and their prayers would be answered.

Now only the soldiers were here, but I saw new rolls of paper in the holes. And now only the soldiers and our little congregation from Mount Zion were praying at this Wall—on the first Sabbath eve that the Old City was in Jewish hands after nearly two thousand years.

After the outpouring of prayers which came from the depth of the heart, prayers of thanksgiving and praise, they joined hands and, with their eyes wet, they danced and sang. Their joy seemed to enter into the very stones of the Wall, dry the well of tears and hush the wails of anguish collected within it over the centuries.

I watched Raymond, the 'gentile from the nations', being caught up by that little band of dancers and singers. They drew him lovingly into the Jewish family. My thoughts took flight into the future depicted in a Psalm of David, when *all nations whom thou hast made shall come and worship before thee, O Lord, and shall glorify thy name*.

It was such a significant moment in our history. We realized how privileged we were to be present at this special Sabbath service. We were still dazed for it was an experience which could never be described in words. Things of the spirit can only be apprehended by the spirit. Only according to the measure of the spirit given to us can we in turn measure the importance of a spiritual event. And only by faith can we see into the future revealed by the spiritual event.

The soldiers at the Wall produced some wine and cakes for the blessing and thanksgiving in which we all joined. Then we started on our walk back to Mount Zion. It was now very dark. Our Nahal boys guided us back with the same loving care and we were all in a state of spiritual exultation. We returned safely to our home and continued the celebration for a while.

*   *   *

Police barriers were going up in places of danger. The soldiers were still around, but all was quiet, and there was a sense of peace once again on Mount Zion.

Albert went, as usual, to the morning service at the little synagogue. The same small faithful band of worshippers as before were present. After the service they all came back to the house for 'kiddush'.

It was a joyous reunion. Many wet eyes but such happy faces. After the blessing on the wine and the recounting of experiences, they all joined hands and danced and sang songs of praise. 'It was surely a God-given miracle,' they said.

The previous Sabbath Rabbi Twilensky had told us about a very holy man, a shoemaker, who was regarded as one of the saints—the traditional thirty-six saints who uphold Israel before the throne of God. He had died a year ago and left a letter which was not to be opened until the Feast of Lag B'Omer. This letter foretold that war was imminent, but that it would only last a few days and end in a great victory for Israel. . . .

The prophecy had been fulfilled between this and the previous Sabbath.

The Week After

We were still having trouble with the water supply; not only was it limited but the pressure was terribly weak. I walked round the garden. It was parched and gasping with thirst, yet we had to collect the trickle of water there in buckets for our needs in the house. We were so grateful for these drops of water.

I recalled the last days of the Siege of Jerusalem in 1948 when we had waited in queues for the water-carts to come through the streets, risking bullets and shells in order to collect our small ration. When the water was running so low that we could not have held out for more than a few days longer—the miracle occurred. A new road was made, enabling a convoy to come through bringing food and water to the besieged city at the last moment. Another miracle. . . .

Now we at least had water for our urgent needs, and the damaged pipes would soon be repaired so that water could once again flow through freely.

Life was beginning to return to normal. We could go out shopping. Yona and Paulita returned to Mount Zion and the pigeons had returned to their old roosting-places. They had been frightened into hiding during the noise of battle. The workmen appeared again and we heard the familiar sound of rubble being thrown out on to Garden Square from the window of an old building under repair— a noise that had been going on at its own slow pace for the past year.

It was hard to believe that we had experienced a war. Only the occasional explosions, the broken fence on the border and the new road reminded us of that fact.

Work had been going on at a frantic pace on the new road from Mount Zion to the Old City—to the Wall. It was to be finished for the following day, the eve of Shavuot when it would be opened officially for pilgrims going to the Wall.

There were many explosions that day, but they were not all mines. The houses in the area facing the Wall were being demolished, making room for the hundreds of thousands of people who would be coming there. There has been much controversy about the opening up of this space. Some felt it was a great mistake to demolish the surrounding houses, and felt it deeply enough to have shed tears over it. Others say it would have been quite impossible to leave it as it was, with only a small space open before the Wall, to allow for the countless pilgrims who would now be visiting there.

I was glad that I had been able to see it again as it was, when, in the midst of the old houses, one was suddenly confronted by the enormous stones of the Wall, stones which impressed one with a sense of timelessness, change-lessness. Only the precincts of the Wall could change, for the stones themselves remained as they were at the time the Temple had been built.

The road was asphalted and ready. Police barricades were being erected everywhere so that people could only go in the direction of the Wall, and not enter any other area. Detours off the road were prohibited since the surrounding fields were full of mines.

The road was to be opened at dawn the next morning. But people from all parts of Jerusalem were converging on Mount Zion on the eve of Shavuot, even before the first stars had appeared in the sky. All the surrounding open spaces were filling up and many were seeking places in the parks to sleep. Everybody wanted to be as near as possible as early as possible for that great pilgrimage to the Wall in the Old City.

Many of the very orthodox were wandering around Mount Zion, impatient in their eagerness for the road to be opened. All through the night, singing voices could be heard. Songs of joy, prayers of praise and thanksgiving. There were also voices crying out in anguish for their lost ones, whose blood was hardly dry in the streets of the Old City. That night heaven and earth seemed to clasp hands. I looked up at the dark sky, shining with stars. Some unusual white clouds were strewn across the sky. Were they clouds? Or were they the outspread wings of the celestial guardians of Mount Zion under which the Children of Israel were gathered?

Shavuot Pilgrimage, 1967

The dark night sky slowly changed to a delicate transparency with the first pale rays of dawn, as I watched and listened from our balcony. It was the morning of Shavuot.

Shadowy figures were gathering round the entrance to the road. The flags of Israel hung almost motionless on their poles. Even the breeze stood still on this momentous morning. The singing, chanting and crying of the night had died down. Voices were hushed and footsteps rang out more clearly.

The pale, translucent sky was changing colour. Behind the Mount of Olives and the mountains of Moab, facing us, it was steeped in flaming crimson. A little procession of people walked towards the entrance of the road. The Chief Rabbi recited a prayer. At last the barrier was removed; the road was open.

The first pilgrims had started silently on their way to the Wall when we went down to join them. A stream of people that was to continue unbroken for the two following days and nights.

Albert and I walked with them, the people of Israel—men, women and children of all ages, from all communities: the extreme orthodox, the free thinkers, and those of every shade of belief in between. Babies in arms, babies in prams, people in wheelchairs, a man with one leg, and an old man in a prayer shawl, running as though the spirit was driving him, his prayer shawl flapping like wings. It was a very orderly, quiet and dignified procession, and on every face there was an expression of joy, happiness and awe.

With the road finished, the walk was much easier than it had been on the previous Friday evening, but as we passed through the Dung Gate we did not recognize where we were. The houses and alleys in the approach to the Wall had completely disappeared and a great open space revealed the whole of the Wall at one glance.

The whole atmosphere had changed. Before, each separate stone had made an impact on one's consciousness. Now the stones were but part of the structure of the Wall, and the Wall itself just a small fragment of the original outer Wall of the Temple. Before, it had stood so symbolically enclosed and hidden by alien walls, profaned and bereft of the proximity of any worshipper. Now it stood freed, revealed, welcoming the present generation of Abraham's descendants to the place where Abraham proved his obedience to God and where he had received the promise: '*In thy seed shall all the nations of the earth be blessed.*'

The large, open Square filled up gradually with thousands of pilgrims on this morning of Shavuot. Torah Scrolls were placed before the Wall and everyone prayed—some silently, some aloud, believers and unbelievers. Passing close to the Wall, some kissed the stones and made them wet with tears. Others touched them with their hands, feeling a need for physical proof that it was no dream.

It was a sacred moment for those faithful souls who had dreamed all their lives of this fulfilment. And those who had always felt themselves immune to any religious or specifically Jewish feeling were surprised to find that there were cracks, widening cracks in the walls of indifference, which they had built up around themselves.

This was an historic day. Together with the Children of Israel gathered in that place near where the Temple had once stood were the invisible hosts of heaven—the armies of God. And the prayers, mounting on clouds of wings, ascended to the throne on high.

From our window on Mount Zion, where we had always looked out on to the iron fence marking the border with the enemy military post behind it, we now watched the constant flow of people passing along the road to the Wall —a quiet, joyous, thankful Israel.

Before, we had been right at the end of the new city; now we were in the centre of a united Jerusalem—old and new made one. Mount Zion and Mount Moriah, with no barriers between.

Throughout the day the human stream flowed gently past our window. It was a hot day and many stopped on their way to rest a while and have some refreshment at Ha-Ohel. In everyone there was a happiness which seemed to lift them off their feet as though they were hovering slightly above the earth.

Epilogue

It is now over five years since the barriers dividing Jerusalem were removed, and Jews and Arabs have been able to mingle freely, although the battle for lasting peace has not yet been won.

The scene on Mount Zion is constantly changing. As I look through our window on this sunny summer day I see the tourist buses filling the Pope's Parking Lot, the cars filling Garden Square, and large groups of tourists—their numbers are ever increasing—following their guides into the souvenir shop. I hear many different languages being spoken: French, German, English, Italian, Dutch and many unfamiliar tongues as well.

Mingling with the endless groups of American, English and German speaking tourists are dark-skinned women from Africa with their colourful robes and head-scarves. Moving among the mini-skirted westerners are Indian women in graceful saris. Some Japanese tourists have become entangled with a group of nuns. Most of them stop and peer through the iron railings where the steps lead down to our garden, and all take photos.

Beyond our garden fence, a camel complains loudly at having to stand up to be photographed with a tourist on his back. Groups of Arab boys accost the tourists, trying to sell their wares: postcards, wooden bead necklaces, reed flutes, drums and other souvenirs. There are very small boys who sell chewing-gum and acid drops.

An Arab has brought a donkey and loudly recommends a ride on its back down to the Wall. Another Arab youth is to be seen walking among this press of people with his pet lamb at his heels, and calls out to draw the attention of generous tourists to its faithfulness. Goats are grazing between the stones all around.

Then there are the Arab women with their beautifully embroidered long dresses and white head-scarves flowing down their backs, who pass the Pope's Parking Lot going down the road to Silwan. On their heads they carry baskets of vegetables or fruit.

A few long-haired, strangely dressed young men with shaggy beards are sitting on the steps at the entrance to a restored building, now an American Yeshiva (religious school), and known locally as the 'Hippie Yeshiva'. They are singing religious songs to the accompaniment of a guitar.

The threats of renewed hostilities expressed by our neighbours neither limit the ever-increasing influx of tourists nor dampen their spirits. The throbbing pulse of the dynamic life of Jerusalem can be felt here on Mount Zion.

The ceaseless noise of the day now intrudes also into the night: buses bring loads of tourists to be entertained with Israeli and Chasidic songs sung to the loud beat of drums and other instruments. Only in the early morning hours, before the noisy activity of the day begins, can the peace of Mount Zion still be felt.

On one such morning I went down into the garden to help Butros with the watering. He is a young Christian Arab who has been helping me with the garden since 1968. His sincerity and kindness have never failed. His dark eyes are always alight with warmth and his friendly smile and cheerful humour have so often changed a moment of heaviness into laughter and good cheer.

On this early summer morning, we were surprised to see a large taxi stop at the Pope's Parking Lot. We looked over the stone wall of the garden and saw an Arab driver get out of his car. He appeared to be the only occupant. He opened the boot of the car, and to our amazement, began lifting out lambs. . . .

'One, two, three . . .,' counted Butros, and continued with surprise, 'four, five, six, seven, eight!'

'Look,' I exclaimed, as he then opened the door of the car, and we watched another six sheep jump out. He gathered them all together and took them to the green patches near the wall on Mount Zion to find their breakfast.

Butros and I laughed.

'You see,' said Butros, 'it is so good now that we have peace, even the sheep ride to Mount Zion in a car to seek holy food.'

A short while afterwards, we saw the Arab return with his passengers to the taxi and drive away.

'Everything happens on Mount Zion, Butros,' I said, as we finished the watering and he left to go to his regular work near by.

Before I entered the house, my first visitor had arrived. Coming up the road from Silwan was a man carrying a large bunch of flowers in one arm and a basket filled with freshly picked green figs in the other hand.

'Good morning, my sister,' he said, as he reached the gate. 'I have brought you these things from my garden.'

'How kind of you, Achmoud,' I said, as I greeted my good friend and Arab neighbour. 'But why so much?' I chided him.

'Because you are my sister,' said Achmoud. 'You must get the first and the best from my garden, and I know how many people come to you here.'

I was always deeply moved by this generous expression of friendship, but I had learned in these last few years of contact with the Arabs that when they like someone, their generosity knows no bounds. We chatted, Achmoud and I, over a cup of Turkish coffee, before he rose to go. The daily life of Mount Zion had not yet begun.

* * *

I remembered the beginning of our Brotherhood of Goodwill in 1965. Then I had dreamed of having Arabs in our

midst. Now the dream had come true. People of goodwill
from all circles and nations had met at Ha-Ohel and over
the years had grown together, bound by the spirit of goodwill, faith and love. We welcomed our Arab brethren.

* * *

With the awakening of another day, I heard the first bird
call and then the answering chorus, as I went down as usual
into the garden to savour its peace. On this June morning
as I tended to the plants, I remembered the dream garden
as I had first planned it in my mind. Its realization had been
beyond all expectation.

I looked at the fruit trees. We had filled baskets with
delicious golden loquats each day for weeks. Now the
peaches were tinted with pink and swelling in the warming
sun. The little green nut pods were growing fast on the
almond tree which had blossomed early this spring. Next
to it the dainty pomegranate tree was gaily decorated with
orange-coloured flowers. Large clusters of grapes hung from
the vines climbing up the walls. There would be an abun-
dance of plums, olives and mulberries, and the orange tree
in front of the house was heavy with fruit—some of it gold,
the rest still green.

In this comparatively small garden of not more than two
hundred square metres, we now had about the same number
of different flowers, shrubs and trees. During the eight
years we had been in the house I had received seeds, bulbs,
plants and cuttings from the many interested visitors who
had come to Ha-Ohel from so many different countries.
Planted, these gifts had invariably flourished, even the
delphiniums which took six years to adapt themselves
to the new conditions, but are now the pride of the
garden.

I looked at the fuschias, brought from Germany, growing
in the half-shade under the orange tree. Their dainty foliage
was fringed and dotted with hanging bells—purple and red,

white and pink, each pendant trumpet with its petals delicately upturned.

The beautiful pink, dark-spotted tiger lily stood tall and proud, displaying eight magnificent flower heads on one heavily laden stem. Close by, a red-and-white striped amaryllis lily lingered, as though loathe to depart. Agapanthus were just beginning to show the small green sheaths enclosing buds which would later burst into glorious sprays of blue flowers.

A covering of purple bougainvillaea softened the corner of the wall behind the roses. Masses of red bougainvillaea formed an arch over the steps leading down to the garden, while the golden-pink variety trailed in profusion over the railings on top of the garden wall in front of the house.

It is in this corner that the jacaranda tree stands so tall, its spreading branches giving shade all around. I looked up and saw the mists of mauvey-blue resting on the fernlike leaves—the myriads of flower bells, softly glowing in the early morning sun. At its foot the shade-loving, delicately tinted aquilegia grew side by side with the flowering cactus whose native home is in the stony desert sand. In a sunny corner, tritoma thrust flaming spear heads in front of the Peace rose covered with pink-tinged yellow blooms. I gazed at the delphiniums in all their different shades of blue, from the palest hint of colour to the deepest purple.

As I was contemplating the miracle of this mixture of flowers from so many different countries with different climatic conditions, all growing in such happy profusion, someone came into the garden beside me. It was Ibrahim, an Arab gardener who had created and tended for over twenty-five years what was held to be the most beautiful garden in East Jerusalem. He came often to see this garden and we exchanged seeds, seedlings and experiences.

'How is your garden, Ibrahim?' I asked.

'It is very beautiful now,' he replied, 'but nothing like yours. Everything here somehow seems to grow better and flower longer. I've never seen a garden like this.'

He had also never seen the one flower we were now watching daily, the crowning glory which I had never expected to have in our garden—the exotic strelitzia. A group of these plants had been given to me when they were three years old. Due to bloom in their fifth year, I had lovingly cherished them, waiting for the first flower.

The first bud had appeared a month ago and was slowly unfolding its rare beauty. Known as the 'crane flower' or 'bird of paradise', it bears a remarkable resemblance to the regal head of a bird with a rich golden crested crown, and a deep-blue long, pointed beak above its grey, green and gold-lined throat.

Ibrahim and I looked at it in wonder. This morning it had opened its strong long beak and I felt that at any moment a loud call would ring forth—a call to remind us that one day paradise would again be here on earth.

After Ibrahim had left, I sat on the old stone bench under the mulberry trees where the lawn was like a soft green carpet under my feet. Seen through the curtain of flowers inside the garden wall, the hills of the Judean desert already looked brown and parched. The hot dry wind blowing from the desert—the hamsin—had been frequent this spring.

I heard footsteps coming down the path. David, a friend from London who had been staying with us for some days, came to join me in the garden.

'The air seems to have been sprayed with a special perfume this morning,' he remarked.

'Yes,' I replied, 'the garden always has supplies of perfume, handed on from plant to plant as the seasons change. It begins with the hyacinths in the spring and passes on to the freezias, roses, stocks and other scented flowers as the season advances.'

'I remember the orange and lemon blossoms when I was here the last time. They really seemed to drench the night air with their scent.'

'Well, this morning it's the turn of the sweet-scented jasmine hanging over the wall behind the roses,' I pointed out.

We sat for a while in silence adding our prayer of thanksgiving to the unseen cloud which seemed to rise heavenwards like incense from every little flower in the garden.

David had arrived from London the previous week when the wave of violence and terror which had rolled over the earth from far-away Japan had reached its destined target—Lydda airport.

He had escaped injury, but had witnessed the scene of murderous horror when three young Japanese travellers, working for the Arab terrorists, had taken machine-guns out of their suitcases and fired indiscriminately into the crowd of pilgrims, tourists and returning Israelis gathered in the customs hall. In all, twenty-six people were killed and another seventy wounded—innocent men, women and children.

It was one of the most horrifying manifestations of the spiritual darkness and confusion which now covers almost every corner of the earth.

David had come to us in a state of shock. He had spent many hours resting in the garden, and as he sat beside me now he asked: 'Do you know that in England we say the nearness of God can be felt in a garden more than in any other place on earth? I think I feel the presence of God here more than in any other garden I've ever been in.' He went on, 'Each day as I sat in this garden I could feel its peace and healing envelop me. I felt the Presence so close that there were moments when I was almost overcome by a feeling of awe.'

I thought of the many different people who had been in this garden and who had described similar experiences. The garden had fulfilled its purpose: there was not only its peace and healing quality but also something within it of the spirit of Mount Zion.

On the day David returned to London, a week later, the post brought a letter from friends living near New York. Arnold and Ruth, who had their own beautiful home and garden, came to Israel every year in the early summer for three or four days. The sole reason for their visit was to spend the time with us in Ha-Ohel.

Ruth had written: 'We are shocked by the Lydda massacre. The state of the world today makes it hard to retain one's faith and peace of mind. When I begin to feel discouraged or depressed, then I want to come to your beautiful garden and feel once more the tranquillity and find new courage to go on.'

*   *   *

At the end of the day, when the sun had turned off its golden light and the noise had ceased, I walked up to the open Square where the pine trees seemed to bend their outstretched branches even lower than usual—perhaps in sadness, perhaps in prayer.

I sat on the bench beneath the trees, the same bench where I had sat when first I came 'to walk about Mount Zion' to search for a place to make a garden and a home, and I thought of the vision and promises for the future of Mount Zion. It was on that bench I sat, and sought to understand the will of the Lord concerning our coming to live on Mount Zion.

So much had changed since then, so much gained and so much lost. In the midst of all the noise it was hard to hear the voice of Zion, the message of Zion, but now in the stillness, as the stars began to sparkle through the bowed pine trees, I sensed the spirit of Zion, its power and strength.

I felt again that infinite peace—a peace born of prayers

that lingered and tears that had spent themselves. A peace deep in the heart of Mount Zion, assured of its glorious future.

> *'When the Lord shall build up Zion,*
> *He shall appear in all His glory.'*
>
> Psalm 102

Jerusalem, June 1972